David Grant is the aut
as a vet. He studied at
University, and Edinburgh University, before working on
a farm practice when he first qualified, and then at the
RSPCA Harmsworth hospital as a junior vet. After a year
in Colombia he only just survived the culture shock of
working as a vet in Chelsea. He has been director of the
RSPCA Harmsworth hospital since 1987, now a venue for
the hugely popular *Animal Hospital* series. He is married
with two children and lives in London.

Also by David Grant

Tales from the Animal Hospital
A Year in the Life of the Animal Hospital
Just Practising
Still Practising

¡Viva El Vet!

From the Animal Hospital
to a Colombian Practice

DAVID GRANT

**POCKET
BOOKS**

LONDON · SYDNEY · NEW YORK · TOKYO · SINGAPORE · TORONTO

First published in Great Britain by Simon & Schuster UK Ltd, 2001
This edition first published by Pocket Books, 2002
An imprint of Simon & Schuster UK Ltd
A Viacom Company

Copyright © David Grant, 2001

The right of David Grant to be identified as author of this work
has been asserted by him in accordance with sections 77 and 78
of the Copyright, Designs and Patents Act, 1988.

1 3 5 7 9 10 8 6 4 2

Simon & Schuster UK Ltd
Africa House
64–78 Kingsway
London WC2B 6AH

www.simonsays.co.uk

Simon & Schuster Australia
Sydney

A CIP catalogue record for this book is available from the British Library

ISBN 0–7434–0903–5

Typeset by Palimpsest Book Production Limited,
Polmont, Stirlingshire
Printed and bound in Great Britain by
Bookmarque Ltd, Croydon, Surrey

Although all the stories that feature in this book are true,
the names of pets and owners have been changed to protect their privacy.

To Gloria M and Gloria S
with love as always

Acknowledgements

With thanks to Helen Gummer, Katharine Young, Glen Saville and all the staff at Simon & Schuster. Special thanks go to Pepsy Dening and Julian Alexander.

Chapter 1

'David, sorry to bother you, but do you think you could come down?'

Andy, the Harmsworth's in-house philosopher, and one of the small team of drivers who manned the phones, was his usual cool, unrattled self. But I knew this was an emergency. It was gone midnight and I was thinking of going to bed. The long winter nights dragged, especially when I was on call. I put on my shoes and took the fireman's route to the floor below, down a purpose-built ladder hidden behind a door in the corridor opposite mine.

I arrived in Reception to find Andy talking to a man standing beside a black Labrador. Well-dressed, in a heavy overcoat with an astrakhan collar, he wasn't the usual sort of client I saw in the RSPCA clinic whose constituency could in general be described as the poor of north and east London – people who could not afford the services of a vet in private practice.

Any doubts I might have had were dispelled when he introduced himself as Lionel Miller, consultant physician based largely at a local hospital. After returning from the theatre that night he had found Portia in terrible pain. Three days before, she had been hit by a car when out walking. He had taken her to his own vet, who had said there was no serious damage. But clearly that was no longer the case: Portia was groaning and her abdomen was very swollen. He had telephoned his vet first, he assured us, but there had been no reply so he had decided to bring her to the Harmsworth.

I was pretty sure I knew what the problem was, but the first thing to do was stabilise the dog. I asked Dr Miller to help me carry her into the operating room where I immediately put her on a drip.

'All right if I stay?' he asked. It wasn't RSPCA policy to involve owners but as he was a doctor I decided he was more likely to be a help than a hindrance.

I quickly put a needle into her abdomen to find out just what we were dealing with. 'Urine,' I said, as the syringe filled with yellowish fluid. 'It looks as though she's ruptured her bladder.' It was a good thing he had brought her in. As it was, I would have to move fast if she was to survive.

Just at that moment, when I was telling him what was wrong and what I planned to do, every light in the building went out.

It was November 1973 and the start of what newspapers were already calling the Winter of Discontent. It was a period of galloping inflation, the price of oil had quadrupled and the miners were on what was called a work-to-rule, in effect an overtime ban. To save electricity, random power cuts were made all over the country. Sometimes we had warning, sometimes not. Like tonight.

The dark of the operating theatre was suddenly enriched by what in those days my mother called 'language' from both me and the doctor. I knew there was no way the labrador would survive till the lights came on again. I would just have to cope as best I could.

The phone was by the door and luckily I remembered I was standing next to it. I reached out, fumbled, found the receiver and picked it up. Andy would be upstairs by now. He answered immediately.

'Andy, it's a ruptured bladder so it can't wait. I'll have to go ahead,' I told him. In fact, I was pretty sure Andy knew that already. There was little the drivers didn't know and their diagnosis was usually spot on. 'I don't suppose you've got any spare lamps up there, have you?'

Tony Self, director of the Harmsworth since my arrival a couple of years before, had risen to the challenge of the emergency and we now had a supply of miners' lamps, which, as Andy remarked, was the ultimate in irony given the miners' role in the emergency.

'Sorry, David,' he replied, 'but there's enough candles to light a cathedral.'

'Don't worry. But I am going to need a hand. Terry up there, by any chance?' Terry was tall and around my age. I would need him to hold one of the lamps as high as possible – a tiring business not suited to someone like Andy who was a good deal older.

First I lit the two candles that Mary, the head nurse, always made sure were on the table by the door. Once that was done I was able to go next door to the prep room and find the lamps, which were fuelled by small canisters of butane gas.

'Anything I can do?' the doctor asked, as I brought back the first.

I handed him a box of matches and went to fetch the others. Thank goodness I'd decided to let him stay.

In a few minutes, with the help of the doctor, we had three lamps going: one for general illumination, which we put on the anaesthetic machine, one held by Terry, who had materialised from upstairs, and one by Dr Miller.

One thing I suddenly remembered that we used electricity for was clipping. No chance of that. In order to clear the hair from the area of incision, I had to resort to that old-fashioned surgical instrument, a razor blade, a supply of which Mary had got in for just that purpose I had discovered. First I soaped Portia, then shaved her. Fortunately Labradors don't have much hair on their underbelly and within a couple of minutes I was ready to start.

The next thing was to get Portia under anaesthetic. No problem with electricity here, just a simple system of valves for the oxygen supply. Dr Miller could be in charge of this side of things, I decided, it being the role of a nurse in usual circumstances.

'I suppose you don't want to scrub up?' I asked him.

'No,' he said firmly. 'I think I'll just hold the lamp.'

That was fine by me.

'But I will need you to hold her head, while I get the anaesthetic tube down,' I explained. While Portia drifted off to sleep I went to scrub up.

'You don't wear a mask, then,' the doctor said, when I began work.

'Not usually. Very little wound breakdown,' I explained. While humans are obviously vulnerable to disease from other humans, the same risk doesn't apply between us and other species.

By now Portia was sleeping peacefully. All Dr Miller had to do to keep her that way was follow instructions, which involved changing the level of anaesthetic gas via a simple dial. We started at level one. 'If I want you to go deeper I'll tell you.' That would involve going up to level three.

I opened Portia up by making a small cut with a scalpel blade. The table immediately flooded with urine – it was pouring out, very nearly a couple of litres. Usually I would have used a suction machine to take it out, but that's another thing that runs on electricity. Nothing I could do now, we would have to clear up later. Just had to be careful I didn't slip.

'Turn the dial up to level two,' I said.

By now the cause of Portia's distress was obvious. Once I'd pushed the abdomen down and found the bladder, I could see a big hole in it. Just a question of stitching it up, but it took twice as long as it would have done had I been able to see properly. Every time my two lamp-holders breathed, the shadows moved and sometimes I was stitching in the dark. Two hours after we started, Portia was back on a drip.

I told the doctor to go home and sleep. I should have done the same thing, but I wanted to keep an eye on Portia. Andy gave me a look, as if to say, 'Do you want me to do it?' I shook my head: the circumstances were so unusual that I didn't want to risk anything going wrong.

I put the Labrador in a cage, pulled a chair in from the prep room and settled down with the latest John le Carré thriller. The next day I phoned Dr Miller as agreed to tell him the good news. She was awake and alert and would make a full recovery.

The most irritating thing about the power cuts was that you could never be sure when they were coming. At first we thought the 'emergency', as it was called, would blow over within a couple of weeks, but two months later on 9 February, the miners' overtime ban became a full-blown strike.

Tony Self was one of those people who always thrived in a crisis. Not only had he come up with the idea of the miners' lamps, he made sure we were kept informed as to when the power cuts – which, when they were planned, usually lasted three hours – were coming.

We were soon down to six hours a day. Heating wasn't a problem, though we made sure that the animals' cages were provided with extra blankets for warmth at night. Neither did consultations cause difficulties. Our major problem was surgical procedures. Although it was perfectly possible to operate without electricity, as my experience with Portia had shown, it was more risky, particularly if broken bones were involved. To ensure the best possible diagnosis we would always X-ray before operating. And, of course, X-ray machines run on electricity.

As many of the cuts came in mid-morning, after the early-morning drain on power, Tony Self decided to move operating to the afternoon when the call on the grid was at its lowest and the clinic opened at ten rather than two.

Not that this always worked. I remember one late afternoon in mid-February when I was operating on a cat's femur and the power went. The cat was a black and white male called Spike, a true London moggy with the look of a waiter. The owner had brought him in at about eleven that morning, with the bone protruding through the skin. He had been run over and managed to make his way back to where he lived on three legs. I had taken X-rays immediately as before operating I needed to check that Spike's spine was still intact, see if there were other injuries and look at the chest to see if there was any haemorrhage.

So far so good. Then I put Spike on a drip and went to have a bite to eat at the pub over the road. It had been a particularly full clinic and I needed a break. We had as many consultations as ever which, in those days, meant a hundred a day; split between the two vets on duty, that meant forty or fifty each. Tony Self had decided that we shouldn't restrict ourselves to emergency treatment, but we had to keep our list under control, otherwise we'd be swamped. Although this presented problems, our policy remained to see all cases, emergency or not. Working like this, not knowing how long we had to do anything, put a huge strain on everybody.

Spike would be all right for an hour, I decided, and we'd had no warning about cuts today. Famous last words. No sooner had I clipped the cat's leg than the lights went off. Although it was only shortly after two o'clock, the sky outside was asbestos grey and it was threatening to snow: I could see very little. Our few portable lamps were spread around the building and on this occasion I had only one. By now we had a routine. My nurse that day was Betty and she went straight into the prep room to get a lamp. However, we weren't the only people operating.

Tony had recently become interested in eye operations on dogs and pulled rank, taking three of the available six lamps. Reception had one, and one was for general use in the wards, which left one for me that poor Betty had to hold aloft. For general light we made do with a selection of Price's household candles.

Tony Self was like the David Niven of the vet world, just seemed to lap it up, shouting orders, directing the action. He was like a general in a war film and we were the hapless young officers trying to keep up with him. And his attitude was infectious. Instead of 'Jerry at half past three,' we had 'Lights are going out in five minutes. Get this fellow X-rayed quick. Get this fellow stitched up and into his cage quick. Bop. Bop.' It really was like being in a war. We had to keep going, doing whatever operations we felt needed to be done.

Spike mended well. But elation at a job well done in difficult circumstances could all too easily disappear, particularly when I got back to the flat, exhausted after an afternoon of operations carried out at breakneck speed, to no lights and no music. The obvious answer was to go out, but although there were always pockets of light and entertainment, it was hard to know where to find them. More than one film was spoiled for me by the power failing half-way through.

The most depressing part was that my love-life was also on the wane. Although nothing had been said, I had the feeling that my Colombian girlfriend, known by the drivers on the switchboard outside office hours as Gloria 2, was beginning to distance herself: it was a good few months since she had spent the weekend at the flat and she sometimes took several days to reply to my calls. I had the distinct impression I was on the way out. Either that or she was playing hard to get. I was quite happy to admit that I didn't understand women. Admittedly she had recently taken to talking about friends of hers who had had children and what did I think of children. Needless to say, my response had been pretty negative. Although I was twenty-nine I felt ten years younger, and settling down was a long way from what nineteen-year-olds thought about. The finality of commitment is hard to deal with at that age.

The name Gloria 2 was used for diplomatic reasons by the drivers to distinguish between her and Gloria 1, with whom I had a platonic relationship and who I continued to see regularly. Unfortunately Gloria 2 was in Colombia on an extended family visit and wouldn't be back for several months. So, nine times out of ten I would take myself to the Carpenters Arms, a pub round the corner run by a nice couple. The landlord was a colourful character and his wife was a very good cook. Somehow they managed to make the most of the blackouts with candles and a wonderful old pianist called Jack. It wasn't the kind of place that drunks were interested in frequenting.

Although the state of the nation was the subject most talked about, from pub to prep room, some people seemed oblivious to the fact that there was a crisis.

Although businesses managed to tick over working limited hours (the emergency was now known as the three-day week) animals weren't about to change the pattern of disease and injury. Even so, some humans seemed unaware of the difficulties the Harmsworth was facing and saw no reason to cut down on less necessary visits, which continued as usual.

One miscreant was Bridey, who had been one of my first 'clients' at the Harmsworth. The more stress we were under, the more animals she seemed to bring in.

One morning I was particularly tired and on edge, having been up all night with a gastric torsion in a bulldog, when Bridey came in, complete with her trademark pram filled with assorted cages and boxes.

'So, what seems to be the trouble, Bridey?' I said.

'It's Max. Look at him.'

I looked at him: eyes, mouth, coat, paws. 'Seems perfectly all right to me,' I said.

'But it's his tail.'

I looked at the tail – not losing any hair. I looked under his tail – perhaps this was some euphemism for his nether regions. Nothing. 'What about his tail?'

'It's got a kink in it.'

Indeed it had, giving him a slightly quizzical air.

I felt it. Nothing wrong at all. 'That's just like it is, Bridey. Gives him character, I'd say.'

'That one has enough bloody character, he doesn't need any more.' She paused. 'So there's nothing you can do for him?'

'No. Because there's nothing wrong with him.'

Bridey was an eccentric who was obsessed with animals – mainly cats.

The history of such individuals is often remarkably similar. They usually start with one stray, then word gets about and every stray in the area gets deposited on their doorstep.

These multi-cat households, as they are termed within the veterinary community, are of some interest as they quickly become breeding grounds for feline diseases and you can see the whole gamut of infectious illnesses within a fairly short period. These cat-ladies often appear unkempt – probably because they spend all their disposable income on feed, vets' bills, and their entire free time on cat matters. They are not remotely interested in what other people think of them. In the evenings they go out trapping cats to get them neutered, and try to find homes for the innumerable cats that they find themselves lumbered with. They are far more dedicated than most vets yet paradoxically can cause harm because they can't say no, and end up with too many cats that they cannot look after properly.

Bridey was an intelligent, literate woman, whose other passion was poetry. In addition to the cats, she had a dog, who accompanied her everywhere, tied up to the pram. Usually there would be nothing wrong with him. In those days, clients of the RSCPA were asked to make whatever donation they could afford. Bridey contributed a small amount of money but always included a poem, which was fine by me. I knew that all her available income went on her cats. These poems usually concerned animals or nature and could be spell-binding when she recited them in her magnificent Irish brogue. We quickly built up a rapport whereby I would learn about infectious diseases in cats and something about poetry, while she had a sympathetic vet who would try to fix whatever problem had surfaced in her feline household.

One night after I had seen Bridey, confirmed that one of her cats had cat flu and the rest would probably get it (treatment, none, except rest and isolation), I was awakened from a deep sleep by Terry: Bridey was in the waiting room.

I looked at the luminous dial of my clock as he spoke. It was two o'clock in the morning. Nothing to do with the cats. Her dog, Sausage, had been run over.

I got dressed, feeling bleary-eyed and cursing my luck to have a night duty with an emergency in the middle of the night. It was comparatively rare, even in the busy seventies, to get a call at this time. Most emergencies – and there weren't many true ones – were over and done with by midnight. As I searched for my socks under the bed I couldn't believe that Bridey could be so careless to allow her little Yorkshire terrier to be run over. Many of the Harmsworth's clients were so careless it was criminal – some didn't even possess a lead for their dogs. But Sausage was always tied to that bloody pram. And, anyway, what the devil was the old woman doing on the streets of London at that hour?

'Trapping cats, no doubt,' I muttered to myself, as I stumbled down the emergency ladder into the hospital all ready to give Bridey a piece of my mind.

But as soon as I saw the little Yorkie I knew something was really wrong. Sausage's mouth was white and trembling. I was pleased I had held my tongue.

Bridey had been asleep and had been woken by the dog whining to go out. She hadn't got dressed, just put on her wellington boots and a coat over her night-clothes and waited as the little dog stood straining over a gutter to do his business – he was constipated, so it seemed – when a car, driven by a drunk in all probability, had come at great speed and clipped him up the backside. He was obviously in great pain.

I put up a drip, gave him a jab of pethidine and sat with him for a while to see if he improved. Bridey meanwhile delved into her overcoat and produced a tiny white kitten. 'I wonder, Doctor, if you'd cast your eye over this little mite while you're about it.'

I opened my mouth to protest and thought better of it. After all, night duties were only once weekly – this one would pass. It's been a motto ever since.

While waiting for poor Sausage to perform, Bridey had heard mewing coming from a rubbish chute on the estate where she lived. Finding the little kitten abandoned, she had quickly put it into her overcoat pocket before returning her attention to Sausage. It was then that the car had come racing round the corner – doing sixty miles an hour at least, Bridey reckoned.

The kitten was about six weeks old, I estimated, and had sticky eyes that could hardly open. 'Cat flu,' I said. 'I'll get you some antibiotic ointment for the eyes and you'll have to nurse him through it.' My heart sank at the thought of the rest of Bridey's menagerie who would certainly now get it.

'Him, is it?' said Bridey. 'Hmmm. Cheaper to neuter at any rate.'

I left her tending the latest addition to her extended family while I went into the prep room where I had put Sausage.

He looked a great deal more comfortable and the colour of the lining of his mouth had improved from the deathly white of half an hour before to something approaching normal. I left him with Helen, one of the Harmsworth's qualified nurses, who was doing a spot of night-duty overtime.

Bridey had refused to go home and had put two chairs together in the reception area, covered herself with a blanket that she had brought with her and settled herself down for a night-time vigil. 'Where's the kitten?' I asked.

She smiled, put her finger to her lips, then pointed to somewhere under the blanket.

I took my leave. But for some reason I couldn't get back to sleep. Eventually I gave up trying, got up at six, showered, and went down to see how Sausage was doing.

He was out of shock so with Helen's help I gave him a quick anaesthetic and took an X-ray: a fractured pelvis, which was less drastic than it sounds. In young dogs – Sausage was around two – these pelvic fractures heal within a month, just with rest. There was no need to do anything. I shook Bridey awake and told her the news. 'Rest is what all three of you need,' I said to her firmly, and persuaded her to go home.

She went blessing me for my devotion – I didn't tell her that it was Helen who had been up all night and that I had gone back to bed. Nevertheless I was promised another poem dedicated to me.

A month or so later, when Bridey appeared, Sausage was trotting at her side, fully recovered. Usually she recited her poems, but this one was written in her large looping hand. 'Would you be having a wireless, Doctor?' she said, rather coyly, as she passed it to me.

I told her I did. I had always liked Bridey's poems but I hadn't known if they were really any good. But apparently they were: that weekend, it turned out, was her radio début. And from these beginnings Bridey was offered a scholarship to study in Ireland. But she never took it up. Reason? Her animals, of course.

'I tried to get the Irish Embassy to pay for the inoculations that the kennels would need, but they wouldn't be hearing of it,' she wrote to me later. 'They said a poor poet like me shouldn't be having animals in the first place.'

They were probably right, but money was unimportant to Bridey. Everything she had went on her animals and as inflation kicked in and the price of pet food rose, the plump woman I had met on my first day at the Harmsworth had become thin and drawn, and her clothes hung off her. Quite simply she wasn't eating enough.

Magda, the Polish ambulance driver who ran the old people's animal collection service, was just as bad. With her it wasn't just animals, it was the old people she met while out on the job. Once, after a trip to the East End with Magda we had dropped in at her basement flat in Hackney. It was full of animals. Most were orphans that had come through the RSPCA. It was always happening – but Tony Self had imposed strict rationing on staff and would have been extremely displeased to see his authority flouted in such a way. I wasn't about to say anything. But, as she pointed out, they all had twenty-four-hour access to a large garden, and with tails wagging and enough purring to link up to the national grid, it was clear they had a happy life.

Chapter 2

I don't think I had ever seen Tony Self so animated as during the Winter of Discontent, and something as inconsequential as the three-day week wasn't going to stop him when it came to his latest enthusiasm: eye surgery in dogs. The year before it had been orthopaedics and his enthusiasm for new techniques in bone-setting had rubbed off on his junior staff. Trevor, my old friend and fellow full-time vet, and I were always trying to outdo each other in the number and type of small animal fractures we treated.

The boss could never stand still. He was a great self-motivator, always putting himself on steep learning curves – a trait I now share. This is one of many things I learned from him without realising it. In the world of veterinary medicine there are an infinite number of diseases and conditions to learn about, and treatments are constantly evolving.

Blindness in dogs and cats – as in humans – takes many forms, but only a few, at least in the early seventies, were amenable to treatment. Many were congenital – progressive retinal atrophy, for example, which was a problem in poodles, among others. Here, all that was needed was an accurate diagnosis, made by examining the back of the eye with an ophthalmoscope. It was extraordinary to see the blood vessels in the retina wither away as the retina lost its function. Once the diagnosis was confirmed nothing could be done. The owner would be given the sad news that their pet was going blind due to a slow, irreversible disease with which it had been born.

In humans, eye conditions can be caught reasonably early as patients usually seek medical help as soon as their sight begins to deteriorate. However, the same is rarely true of cats and dogs. By the time an owner came to see us, it was often the case that the animal concerned was already blind. Both cats and dogs adapt quickly to the lack of sight and soon learn to navigate their own homes without any apparent loss of skill to their owners. It is only when they are out and about and lose their way that their blindness becomes apparent.

Tony became fascinated by the few conditions where sight could be restored. There were two in particular, both involving removal of the lens – an operation known as a lendectomy. The first that Tony explored was cataracts. Sometimes dogs develop them and once the cataract is 'mature' the sight is lost. The second, quite common in fox terriers, is where the lens dislocates itself into the anterior chamber of the eye. This is an emergency condition as glaucoma – increased pressure within the eye – may easily result and leads to blindness.

A few months earlier Tony had returned from an ophthalmic course fired with enthusiasm and he instructed Trevor and me to be on the look-out for suitable cases for him to operate on. He gave us a check list. Sometimes a cataract develops as a result of retinal disease, he explained, in which case there is no point in removing the lens as the dog will remain blind. We were told to check the light reflex, by shining a bright light into the dog's eye; a brisk contraction of the pupil was a hopeful sign that the retina was still functioning. These cases would then be handed over to Tony. Trevor and I were soon examining all dogs for eye problems – as I have explained, they are past masters at adapting to sight loss – and it was surprising how many turned up.

Wednesday afternoons were soon allocated for eye operations and the whole hospital would creep about trying not to make too much noise as the work involved was on a very small scale and needed total concentration. The Harmsworth's main operating theatre windows would be blacked out so as not to provide any distraction by what was going on outside and notices would go up everywhere: 'Quiet! Operation in progress!' It was like the inner sanctuary of a temple, with Tony Self the high priest and Mary, exemplifying all that was best in veterinary nursing, in the role of handmaiden. The quiet was sepulchral, only broken on odd occasions by a loud 'Damn and blast' or 'Hell's teeth'.

However, it was reasonably easy to keep out of the way: Wednesday afternoons were as busy as any other afternoon, which meant a stream of clients from two o'clock until five. While Trevor was keen to learn this new specialism, I was happy to stay clear. Eye diseases held no attraction for me. The only specialist area that was beginning to interest me was dermatology, mainly because the cases were so infuriatingly complex and as few vets seemed to know much about them. Also, eye surgery needed specialised instruments. I have never been a gadget man, but I know this aspect certainly played its part in attracting Tony, who loved gadgets and special tools. These were kept in special drawers safely away from whippersnappers like me. Trevor was also drawn to this side of it I think. The only thing Trevor liked more than thumbing through equipment catalogues, whether veterinary or plumbers' merchants, was playing with the things he bought. He seemed to be converting his house in north London entirely by himself.

Like virtually all young veterinary surgeons he was constantly pushing himself to new heights and having cracked orthopaedics, and seeing the boss doing something new, ophthalmology was an obvious choice for fresh challenges. Another eye condition, which usually caused blindness and could be corrected by surgery, that attracted Trevor's attention was KCS. When he first mentioned it, I was mystified.

'Kerato-conjunctivitis sicca,' Trevor explained. 'Dry eye to you, maestro.'

I frowned while I tried to remember what this condition was all about. We had quite a few dogs under treatment for dry eye, as I still preferred to call it, but I had never considered it in any detail. As far as I was concerned, the tear glands shrivelled up for some unknown reason and stopped producing tears. As a result, the cornea dried up and was prone to infection. If you did nothing, blindness resulted. All we could do was supply false teardrops, which the owner had to put in to the eyes at least six times daily. This becomes tedious after a while, and I always assumed it was a lucky dog who got the full treatment.

Trevor had heard of a new technique, which sounded bizarre to say the least.

'All you have to do,' he explained, 'is transplant the parotid duct from the mouth to the eye. Whenever the dog salivates he automatically lubricates the cornea. Simple!'

I laughed. 'I'll believe it when I see it.'

Almost immediately a case presented itself: a nine-year-old West Highland white terrier who had had KCS diagnosed a few years back.

Diagnosis is easy. We stick a small strip of fine paper into the eye. The paper has number markings on it in millimetres. In normal dogs the tears wet the paper quickly and travel up the strip in less than a minute. In dogs with KCS it is slower. In Snowy's case there were no tears at all and the paper stayed dry. He was owned by two pensioners, and for the first six months Mr and Mrs Watson had done quite well, putting in the drops regularly, but then arthritis took its toll and Mrs Watson – who was at least eighty – had trouble holding the dog's head still and dropping in the 'tears'. Snowy wasn't the most co-operative of dogs and everyone agreed he would be an ideal case for the new operation.

It was set for the following Wednesday. I volunteered to consult on my own while the two ophthalmologists got to work. With a bit of luck they would be finished by four and could help me mop up the rest of the consulting. I decided to start half an hour early – I knew there would already be people waiting, but I was surprised to see Paddy Flynn sitting in Reception. Paddy was a familiar face around the area. He played the accordion near the tube station, the money he collected going to charity. An ancient spaniel called Charley guarded the collecting tin. I had seen Paddy a day or so before when he came in convinced that his dog was dying.

At first sight Charley looked as if he had had a stroke. His head was on one side and he couldn't walk properly. 'If you t'ink Charley's time has come and want to put him down, it'll be hard, mind, but I'll understand,' had been Paddy's opening line.

One of the other possibilities for this imbalance, apart from a stroke, was middle-ear disease and I made sure to look down the ear before thinking of drastic measures. There, plumb in the middle of the ear canal and resting against the eardrum, was a grass seed. I should have thought of it straight away: we were coming into the grass-seed season – July. Soon every other dog with a head tilt would be a prime suspect.

'How old would you say Charley is, Paddy?'

'To be sure, I'm not altogether knowing. Maybe sixteen or seventeen. Would that be near it?' Too old to be having an anaesthetic without a very good reason, I thought.

I decided to see if I could fish out the seed without going down that dangerous route. 'I'll get one shot at this, I reckon,' I said, 'then Charley will get wind that it isn't pleasant and refuse to co-operate.'

Paddy spoke softly to the dog and held his head perfectly still. In the event a large grass seed was on the table in ten seconds, using long forceps – crocodile forceps, so-called because the end opens and shuts like a crocodile's jaws and is useful for grasping grass seeds. Paddy was amazed. Just five minutes previously he was prepared to say goodbye to the companion of his old age and now he had a perfectly healthy dog. He gave a donation of three pounds, said it wasn't half enough and that he would be back later with more. I tried to say that that was entirely unnecessary, but he tapped his nose and left, with Charley trotting happily along beside him. For someone of Paddy's age and income, three pounds seemed the height of generosity.

By now I could hear quite a queue developing in the waiting room and I decided to get cracking. Then, suddenly, I heard the unmistakable sound of an accordion. So this was how Paddy was planning to raise more funds I realised with a wry smile. I looked at my watch. Two o'clock precisely. The eye operations wouldn't get going in earnest for another half-hour. Perhaps by then Paddy would have collected enough money to satisfy himself and be away.

No such luck. Soon seventy or more people and their animals were being entertained in the waiting room and the music showed no signs of petering out. Paddy's first offering had been 'How Much Is That Doggy In The Window', which proved to be a barn-stormer, with the audience joining in. It soon sounded more like a knees-up at a pub than a waiting room at a veterinary hospital. But the animals didn't seem to mind and one song followed another. I wasn't sure what to do about it – if anything, it seemed to cheer everyone up. Instead of gloomy faces at the consulting-room door, everyone was smiling. At three o'clock there was a sudden influx of additional people as customers were kicked out of the neighbouring pub. News had got round that a party was going on.

My main worry was Tony and Trevor, both hard at work on delicate eye operations. I was surprised that neither had stormed out already to pull the plug on the afternoon's entertainment. Tony had popped his head out early on to see what was going on, but just smiled, although later above the din I could just hear a few damn-and-blasts.

It was just before four when Paddy went into the familiar strains of 'When Irish Eyes Are Smiling', which signalled the end of his performance.

Half an hour later two stressed-looking vets came up to the nurses' common room where I was having a cup of tea. 'Nothing to do with me, Guv,' I said, raising my hands like a cowboy who'd just had a six-shooter pulled on him. 'Just a satisfied client's way of saying thank you. And, according to Betty, the clinic is twenty pounds better off.'

I was half expecting a dressing-down, but the boss had a good sense of humour and, more to the point, the operations had gone well. As for Snowy, it was remarkable but true: the simple expedient of moving a saliva gland to his eye so that spit could take the place of tears put an end to the misery of dry eye. The power of lateral thinking.

Eventually life returned to normal in terms of power

supply, but it was many years before anyone dared to get rid of the miners' lamps.

At least now my social life could have some kind of structure. I could go to the cinema or a concert without risking the whole thing going dark half-way through. But my love-life was still in a sorry state. Although I was still seeing Gloria 2, the weekends spent walking on the heath, followed by Colombian bean stew at the flat, were a thing of the past. She had become enamoured of the English countryside and was always disappearing for weekends in Gloucestershire or Hampshire. Looking back, I realise she was dropping heavy hints, always going on about how wonderful life must be for a country vet, but I didn't pick them up. By August, the hit song by a girl group called the Three Degrees seemed all too appropriate: 'When Will I See You Again?'

The one thing in my life that continued to flourish was my study of Spanish, and that May I took my Spanish O level, greatly helped by Bertica Garcia – the wife of my friend and colleague from Colombia, Henry Garcia. Although I spoke Spanish with Gloria 2, it was Bertica who helped me with grammar and steered me through the oral element of the curriculum. It was shortly afterwards that Gloria 2 reopened the idea of me going to Colombia to work. Again, I didn't notice the thrust of her message, which was 'and when you come back you could probably be persuaded to get a job in the country'.

She had first suggested a move to Colombia a year or so before, but now I was beginning to think it wasn't such a bad idea. If I was going to travel I had to do it now. I was definitely growing old. The heroes of my youth – the Beatles, the Stones, the Who, the Kinks – were history: now it was Abba and Donny Osmond. It was enough to make you take up the accordion.

¡Viva El Vet!

*   *   *

The reasons why people have cats and dogs as pets are obvious to anyone, but some pets are less easy to warm to. High in that category for me are hamsters. First, they bite. Never put your finger into a sleepy hamster's cage: he will bite and you will retrieve your finger involuntarily only to have the hamster let go and fall the equivalent of the Eiffel tower. Second, they are only active at dawn and dusk and spend the rest of the day sleeping (or, if disturbed, biting). Third, they have a short life, which, as far as children are concerned, leads to tears.

Hamsters have only been kept as pets since the end of the Second World War. There are over twenty species, the most common being the golden (Syrian) hamster, of which virtually all are descended from three hamsters found in a burrow by an archaeologist near the town of Aleppo in Syria. The name comes from the German, meaning hoarder – they hoard food in pouches in their mouths and, for this reason, mustn't be given sticky foods as this will cause them to get bunged up. Chocolate can kill them, too, as it contains alkaloids toxic to them. Apart from that, in the 1970s I knew little about hamsters. Usually they turned up at the clinic in the company of a small child, but one day in late spring an old man appeared with two seedy-looking specimens, as bald as ageing politicians.

I looked at them – from a distance – and noticed two black spots clearly visible on each flank beneath the thinning fur. 'Hip spots, they are, Guv.' I nodded as knowledgeably as I could. I had never seen such things before. 'What you learned gents call scent glands,' he added. I nodded again, this time with a modicum of understanding. Scent glands are used by many animals to mark territory. Cats have them on their chins. That's why they like to nuzzle you – it's not affection in the conventional sense, simply a way of marking you as their property!

'Nuffink much to do with 'em. In two weeks they'll be dead.'

I asked him why he had that particular time-span in mind.

'It's what they do. At two years and four months they die. And that's next week.'

Admittedly they didn't look at all well, and I decided to go for expert advice from Trevor next door, who was more up in hamsters than I was.

'Demodex probably,' he said. 'Balding like this is a sign of old age – under normal circumstances you wouldn't see the scent glands. Frankly, maestro, they're not long for this world.'

At the mention of demodex, I perked up. My interest in dermatology, although still in the early stages, was increasing. I knew that demodex is a small mite present from birth, which only gets out of hand when the immune system is going downhill.

'So, what's the verdict, then?' the old man asked, when I returned to my consulting room.

'Well, the chances are that this baldness is caused by a mite, but I'll have to do tests, I'm afraid.'

'As you like. But it won't make no difference,' he said gloomily. 'You mark my words, two weeks' time they'll be dead as doorknockers. It's always the same. I've been breeding 'amsters for the last twenty years and it's always the same. Two years four months, curtains.'

When the clinic was over I did skin scrapes and spent a happy half-hour poring over the microscope looking at these cigar-shaped mites. Not that it did much good. In those days there was no cure, so I gave each hamster a multi-vitamin shot, hoping it would give their immune system a boost.

Two weeks later I was passed a message by the duty nurse. 'An old man called to tell you that you're not to take it personally but the two hamsters died. He said to tell you two years and four months precisely.'

That summer the temperature shot up to the eighties and we had a spate of balcony cats. It happened every year, almost like clockwork: half a dozen cats would appear in the cat wards in various states of injury. Their high-rise-living owners kept the balcony windows shut for most of the year, then suddenly the cats had a taste of freedom: not understanding just how high they were, they leaped off the railings and fell like lead.

If the cats were alive by the time they hit the ground, we would nearly always be able to save them. But it was very labour intensive. The old adage about cats always landing on their feet is probably correct, but from a height of up to a hundred feet, this didn't do them any favours. Most of the cats who lived had fractured legs – front or back, depending on how they landed: front feet first, and they would have a broken jaw in addition to two broken front legs. The jaws always broke in the same place – right in the middle – and we had all become adept at wiring them together. I had just finished fixing a jaw one early evening when Magda brought in another.

'That's the second bleedin' one today.' Magda's first language was Polish and she never got the instinct for when the circumstances were appropriate for swearing and when they were not. 'Pardon my French.' This was her standard apology when she thought she might have got it wrong. 'I can't help strong language. Something needs to be done.' Magda was a great campaigner and a great doer. I have never known anyone with so much energy. When she wasn't working with animals she was working with the old people she befriended through her job. 'I've already rung the papers,' she added. 'The next one I get I'm taking a reporter with me.'

'I hope you've got clearance from ADS,' which was how we referred to the boss, whose full name was Anthony Dean Self.

'He won't mind,' she said. 'We've got to stop this carnage.'

Just as we were speaking, a call came through on the radio for a high-rise case in the middle of an estate in Bethnal Green, just east of the City.

'Right,' said Magda, wearing her battleaxe expression. 'I'm on my way.'

A couple of phone calls later and she was gone, stopping on the way to pick up a young woman reporter and a photographer. As it was around five and the clinic would shortly be closed, I told her I'd stick around to see what I could do to help her in her one-woman campaign to save the balcony cats.

It was about an hour later when I got the call. She was on her way back. When she had arrived at the estate nobody had seemed particularly bothered about the cat, a black male, although a box had been placed over him, as instructed by the phone staff. This was routine advice to prevent the injured cat trying to get away and making things worse. Half an hour later she was back at the hospital. Surprisingly the only injury was a broken jaw, no broken legs or serious internal injuries.

I decided to fix it right away. While I was doing this Magda was in full flow to the reporter, Carole. As I worked there was the constant flash of the camera as the photographer took seemingly hundreds of pictures. Over the next few days Tom, as the cat had been imaginatively named by Magda, was coming along quite nicely. A tough East End cat, he had started eating on the second day after his operation.

I had forgotten about the article until the end of the week when a double-page spread was pinned up in the nurses' lounge. There was a large picture of Magda cradling Tom and a smaller one of me wiring his jaw. The caption read: 'RSPCA ambulance driver condemns stupidity of balcony cat owners.' There followed a lot of sensible advice on how to prevent this sort of thing happening.

Within hours of the newspaper being out on the streets the phone calls were flooding in. It was my first taste of what publicity can do to make the general public aware, though I wish I could say that it had any noticeable effect. It didn't. Even now, nearly thirty years later, balcony cats are a regular feature of the Harmsworth's year. The calls that came in that day were divided between people who knew the cat and his owner (who still hadn't come forward to claim his pet), and others who wanted to home Tom.

On my next night duty I met the cat's owner, a curmudgeonly individual whose only concern was the bad publicity he claimed to have had in the newspaper. He arrived a good bit the worse for wear following a session in the pub, demanding his cat back – and even trying to claim that we had taken it without his permission and that we owed him some form of compensation. Magda happened to be on duty and a stand-up shouting match developed with language that made the air go blue.

I expected Magda to get a fist in her face but, amazingly, after a verbal onslaught that would have done justice to a front-line soldier, the drunken man suddenly caved in. 'Keep him, then – if that's what you think,' he roared.

In a flash Magda had a form under his nose and pushed a pen into his hand. She did not soften her language, which was replete with unflattering remarks as to how and when he should leave the building. It was a fearsome performance.

As soon as the coast was clear, Magda embarked on the next stage of her campaign. 'I'm going to 'ave 'im,' she announced. 'That is, if the veterinary surgeon in charge of his case will let him out of the hospital,' she added, fixing me with a you'd-better-agree stare.

I shrugged my shoulders. 'He's signed over and eating. He's all yours, Magda.'

And Tom was added to Magda's menagerie of orphaned animals. I warned her again that if Tony Self found out she'd be in trouble, due to the rule on numbers of pets adopted by staff, for Magda had already far exceeded her quota.

That evening I decided to drop in on Andy and Terry for a coffee and a chat before hitting the sack. A spot of television and that would be it. Their room was just beneath mine. I was feeling gloomy and Andy always had a way of making me feel that all was not lost.

'Oh, there you are,' Terry said, as I walked over to the kettle. 'I tried to call you at the flat but there was no reply.'

'I was with Magda downstairs, we had a bit of a kerfuffle. Didn't you hear it? It nearly ended in fisticuffs.'

We started talking about London, about the lack of care so many people showed to their so-called pets and the impossibility of doing much about it.

'So, what was it you wanted to see me about?' I asked Terry as I was about to leave.

'You had a phone call. Gloria 2.'

¡Viva El Vet!

My heart should have done a little leap, but it didn't. I hadn't seen her for two months because she'd been back to Colombia to see her folks.

'Says to give her a call as soon as possible. Sounded quite mysterious. Good news, she said.'

'Thanks, Terry.' I didn't feel like calling her tonight. Tomorrow would do.

But no sooner had I opened the door than the phone was ringing. I picked it up. Terry again.

'Gloria 2,' he said.

Chapter 3

There are moments in your life when everything changes and you know it. This was one of them. While on holiday in her home town of Medellín, Gloria had decided to investigate the possibility of me getting a job as a vet. When she had first suggested I worked in Colombia, more than a year earlier, I think I had imagined some kind of locum work, something short-term. Perhaps she had too. But that would have been too easy. She had started off by visiting the vet her family had taken their dogs to over the years. It turned out that he had been thinking of moving out of Medellín to work up-country somewhere. In short, he had in mind selling the practice.

He assumed that like all 'gringos' – a term usually applied to Americans who had more money than they knew what to do with – I would have no difficulty in raising the cash. Gloria chose not to disabuse him of this far-fetched idea. She knew only too well that my savings just about covered the fare – and, as she also knew only too well, that the idea of anything permanent was terrifying for one to whom commitment was a no-go area. But, as she kept reassuring me over the next few weeks, there was no long-term commitment, and Eduardo understood that. The idea was simply to go over and try it out. If it didn't work out, it didn't work out.

I had a letter confirming this hare-brained scheme from Eduardo Serrano, the vet. The offer had arrived at just the right time and – tentatively at first – I was persuaded to do it.

But what about visas? And getting my degree validated to enable me to practise in Colombia? I knew from friends that this was sometimes a problem. Gloria just waved her hand in that aristocratic way she had. As long as I had a *palanca*, she explained, everything was possible. *Palanca* – meaning, literally, lever – is a term used to describe somebody with influence. And from what I gathered Gloria's family were wall-to-wall *palanca*.

'In fact, David, without a *palanca* you could not get a job at all.'

The biggest *palanca* of them all – as far as I was concerned – was Gloria's father, Enrique Ruiz. Gloria was curiously reticent about her background – all she had told me was that she was one of six daughters. Henry Garcia, my Colombian vet friend, who had introduced me to her, filled me in. Even by Colombian standards the Ruiz' were very rich, he told me. They hadn't inherited wealth: theirs derived largely from Don Enrique's success as owner of one of the country's biggest fashion department stores. He was also a considerable philanthropist – he had set up an orphanage on the outskirts of Medellín, for example – so he was well known in every sphere of influence.

For the second time in my life I had to pluck up courage to say I was leaving. But, just like my bosses when I left Canterbury, Tony Self made it easy. He said it was a splendid opportunity and of course I should go, that I should keep in touch and, who knows?, I might feel like coming back to the Harmsworth in due course.

Once it was said, I felt quite light-headed. Henry gave me the address of his family: they did not live in Medellín, but if I was ever in a jam I should be sure to call them, he said. Now it was just a question of buying a ticket.

Getting there was the same then as it is today – flying into Bogotá, the capital, then on to Medellín, which lies nearly two hundred miles to the north. I wrote out a cheque to the travel agent for £460, an enormous sum in 1974 – it costs less to fly there now. The ticket was open, I could come back whenever I liked with an option of routes – New York seemed like a good idea.

To celebrate I took Gloria to the little Mexican restaurant in Sloane Square that had given me my first taste of South America. I can picture us now: me with my sideburns, long hair curling over my collar (open), denim flares and sports jacket – a brown check with red threadwork; Gloria with legs that went on and on, wearing a brown velvet skirt that was already not as short as the year before, a tight ribbed polo-neck sweater, her hair in a shining black bob. Black hair would soon become the norm to me, I realised, looking round this restaurant where the majority of women diners were blondes, either real or fake.

Although this was the last time we would see each other for several months, there was no sense of sadness. Indeed, quite the opposite: she was as excited as I was – after all, it had been her idea in the first place – and she chattered on about her family, giving me thumbnail sketches of her sisters and brothers-in-law.

With my ticket safely in my breast pocket, the dream was no longer a dream. That night back at the flat I looked out of my windows across London: it was a view I had come to enjoy. Sometimes after the mayhem of a busy clinic downstairs, I would just sit and stare out at the twinkling lights. It was only just dawning on me that I really was going. I wondered, as I gazed out into the London night, if I would ever again call London home. Tony Self had said that I could always come back to the Harmsworth, but the chances of that seemed remote, whatever happened in South America.

In the meantime I had a month before I was expected in Colombia and I had decided to brush up on my Spanish in Spain.

Colombians pride themselves on speaking the best Spanish in South America. But it is different from European Spanish and, having got used to my Colombian friends in London, it was a bit of a shock to find myself struggling to understand a word in southern Spain. Although the country was beautiful, and the people as friendly as I remembered, there was an air of oppression everywhere: the country was still in the grip of General Franco with the Guardia Civil monitoring our every move – or so it felt. The lack of officialdom that I understood was the way of things in Colombia seemed infinitely preferable.

Having already said my goodbyes at the Harmsworth I spent my final few days before flying to South America in Rochester back at my parents' house. My mother fussed about, complaining that nobody could get into my bedroom because of all the stuff I had crammed in, including my sizeable record collection. I was only taking two suitcases to Colombia, and one of those was half filled with veterinary equipment I thought I might have difficulty getting hold of out there.

Gloria came with me to the airport, full of advice, which I didn't take in, and good wishes to be passed on to her parents, which I did. To anyone else I must have looked like a seasoned traveller – tanned from my three weeks in Spain, smiling confidently and waving good-bye to Gloria – but inside I was a mass of turbulent emotions, excitement at starting a new adventure mixed with vulnerability.

The furthest I had ever flown was two hours to Spain. Now it would be eight hours before we would touch the ground – at Antigua in the Caribbean. Our plane was a Boeing 707, the biggest jet I had ever travelled on. I was lucky to have a window seat, and as I looked down at the patchwork of the English landscape, and recognised the shape of the Isle of Wight as we headed out towards the Azores, I was overwhelmed with homesickness for English fields and weather, English pubs and sense of humour.

Leaving my parents had been difficult – they couldn't understand why I was going. When I told them to think of it as an adventure, they looked blank. Adventures happened in books and films, not in real life. But that was what it was – an adventure, something I had to do. I had no idea of the dangers I was going to face and how the experience would change my life. But as the hours passed I got more excited and less worried – after all, I had a return ticket in my pocket.

I passed the time by reading the guidebook I had bought at a travel bookshop in Notting Hill, which Henry had told me about. Medellín is now notorious as the drug capital of the world, but back in 1974 it was just Colombia's second city, regional capital of an area to the north of the country called Antioquia – in fact, Antioquia was once a country in its own right. Medellín itself is high in the Andes (though not as high as Bogotá) and because it is practically on the equator you can go from a tropical climate to alpine climate within a few miles.

As we approached Antigua I had my first view of a tropical landscape – hills thick with vegetation, pale strips of sand lapped by a deep blue and turquoise sea. Nobody got out of the plane but I stood at the top of the steps while we were being refuelled and experienced my first burst of tropical heat. I had never felt anything like it. The tarmac was shimmering. It was like opening an oven door. And only eight hours away from a distinctly autumnal English morning.

Our next stop was Caracas. A few Venezuelans got off and I could see troops milling around the planes. All had submachine-guns and I could sense an air of menace and violence. Latin-American affairs didn't figure prominently in English newspapers so I had no idea whether this degree of security was normal or whether some conflict was in the offing. I felt relieved when we took off for Bogotá. Twelve hours after leaving London we arrived dead on time.

I had booked my hotel – the Dann – from London; it was where Gloria stayed. I had received so many warnings about being on my guard that I was suspicious of just about everyone, refusing the offer of an airport porter, who looked about twelve years old, and quickly found a taxi with a meter. Not that the meter was ever switched on. Even the driver was a bit of a shock – it was the first time I had seen someone wearing a poncho as normal clothing rather than fancy-dress. With his sombrero he looked like a Mexican bandit.

'Hotel Dann, *por favor.*'

'*Sí*' was the only response I got from him so I jumped into a ramshackle Ford and we sped off. It was early in the morning but even so it was quite cold. I hoped Medellín wouldn't be like this, but then I remembered that Bogotá was very high, some 8660 feet above sea level, compared with Medellín at 5000 feet. I felt quite faint and short of breath – I wasn't used to such an altitude.

The outskirts of Bogotá seemed very run-down. It was a

vast, sprawling place, the houses little more than shacks. Every now and then the taxi would stop at traffic lights and a small army of small children would descend on us with offers of cigarettes, or to clean the windows. They looked young and poor.

'*Gamines*', the taxi driver said, shaking his head. He pointed to his watch, pretended to pull it off his wrist, then gestured to the children as we drove away from them. A flow of incomprehensible Spanish followed and he pointed to his right wrist. I twigged. All drivers wore their watches on the wrist away from the window. Apparently a watch wouldn't last five minutes on the other side.

'*Tenga cuidado*' said the Mexican bandit lookalike, when I paid the fare. 'Take care.' Although the meter had never made a tick, a rough calculation told me I owed him a pound. If everything was that cheap, I'd have no problem, I thought.

My flight to Medellín wasn't till the next day, so I set off to explore, with warnings ringing in my ears from the hotel staff not to wander around in the dark. My first impression of the city was the unfamiliar mixture of smells, the overriding one being petrol fumes – pollution at a level I had never experienced before. Fit though I was, walking about was hard work due to the altitude, and I felt lightheaded and dizzy.

My Colombian friends in London were all of Spanish descent. The people thronging the streets here looked dif-ferent: most had the squat features of the *mestizo* – the mixed-race native Indian and Spanish. And, except for suited businessmen, nearly everyone was wearing ponchos.

With the arrogance of youth, perhaps, I didn't feel any fear, just simple curiosity. If anything untoward happened, well, I could always run away from it, I decided. As a former athlete I could outrun any *gamín* – or anyone else, for that matter. After all, only a few years before I had been the Kent hundred-metres champion. My sprint times were still a match for anyone in Colombia, and so as long as they didn't have a gun I'd be safe. Even so, I left my watch at the hotel.

It was cold when I set off for the airport next morning, but although Medellín is less than two hundred miles from Bogotá, I knew its climate was completely different. It is known as the city of eternal spring and the temperature remains at a fairly constant 22°C. It's a short flight from Bogotá to Medellín, less than an hour. The cities are separated by a deep valley so the scenery changed from mountain to tropical rainforest, back to mountain again, and soon we were circling to land.

Even at the airport – not the best place to get a favourable impression of anywhere – Medellín was beautiful and I immediately fell in love with it. High above me, shimmering in the sunlight, were the Andes but all around was an intense luxuriant green.

I couldn't believe how near the city was, literally on the doorstep. To emphasise the point, an ear-piercing scream heralded the arrival of the next jet, which hurtled over nearby rooftops as we reached the main building. Lord knows what it must be like for the inhabitants of those houses, I thought. I was soon to find out: the clinic was directly in the flight path.

I don't know what I had expected, but what I got was nothing short of a reception committee: Dr Serrano, Pilar his wife, Gloria's parents the Ruiz', one of her sisters Irma, and her husband Gustavo, all *paisas*, as the people who live in Medellín and the surrounding area are called. *Paisas* are instantly recognisable by their strong accent –

the English equivalent would be Geordie – used with pride by them.

During the journey to the Serranos' house, which also doubled as the clinic, I took stock of the man who would be my mentor for the next few months. Eduardo Serrano was tiny, a good inch short of five feet, and I felt like a giant beside him in the passenger seat of his old Renault. He was wearing thick prescription glasses, which made it difficult to see his eyes. Overall, he gave the appearance of being rather a sad man. If the car was anything to go by, the practice wasn't exactly booming, and I thought with nostalgia of the partners' cars in Canterbury.

My new boss also had a pronounced beer belly, the consequence, I soon discovered, of a lifelong love affair with *aguardiente* – the Colombians' favourite drink – literally firewater, which they drank as liberally as I did beer.

Pilar was quite unexpected: short skirt, skimpy blouse and more makeup than you would expect to see outside a theatre. To my youthful European eyes, she looked quite vulgar, though I already had the clear impression that she thought herself glamorous. She had made quite a meal of getting into the back of the car, ensuring that her legs had maximum exposure. Even at that first encounter I decided they made a strange couple.

Leaving the airport I had my first experience of Colombian security. At the exit, we slowed down for a military control where a soldier, with pristine uniform, white helmet and rifle, checked everyone's documents. All Colombians had to carry ID with them at all times, a card with their name, date of birth and a thumbprint. In time, Dr Serrano ('call me Eduardo, please') told me, I would have to have one too.

Less than ten minutes after leaving the airport we drew up outside the house, shortly followed by the rest of our party. And party was the word. A bottle was soon on the table in the patio that took the place of a garden at the rear of the house and Eduardo poured me the first of what would be many *aguardientes*. The taste came as no real surprise because most of my Colombian friends in London drank ouzo, the virtually identical Greek drink, which turns milky when you add water to it. Having already experienced Colombian hospitality in London I knew that I had to go easy. The clinic proved to have been a stopping-off point: soon, we were off to Gloria's family's apartment. They lived in the centre of town, and we had come to the clinic first to leave my bags.

I was going to live with Eduardo and his wife – above the shop, as it were. Their area seemed to be middle-class residential. Eduardo's house was quite small with three bedrooms, and I was shown up to the one above the sitting room, which had a shower off it. The maid's room was downstairs behind the kitchen.

Before we set off for Gloria's parents' home, Eduardo was keen to show off his clinic, which lay to the side of the house. He had converted and extended his garage – not unlike many English vets of the time. Huge purpose-built hospitals like the Harmsworth were still some way off.

The drive up to the old garage led to the waiting room-cum-office. On the desk Eduardo showed me, with pride, a card-index system containing details of all the clients – more than a thousand, he said. I was impressed. This wasn't a job with a salary: the only money I got would be what I earned directly from the clients. 'And, of course, Cristina knows all of them personally,' Eduardo assured me. Cristina, the practice nurse, smiled shyly. She was about thirty, large-boned and with the obligatory long dark hair. Vets all over the world depend on their nurses for much more than the general public imagines, and I knew I would need all the help I could get.

Leading off from the office was the consulting room-cum-operating theatre – just the one room, but I was surprised by how well it was equipped: a huge stainless-steel operating table dominated the room and on the bench a new Olympus microscope emphasised that this was a proper clinic.

There were shelves of needles and syringes and boxes of thiopentone – a barbiturate anaesthetic we used at the Harmsworth. I soon learned that intravenous anaesthetic was the only way to render the patients unconscious here. I would have to do without the high-tech anaesthetic machines of the Harmsworth. I had been spoilt, I knew – friends in the profession often told me so – but I had also seen English practices where they relied on intravenous anaesthetics only and I knew that I would be able to adapt. There was a good operating lamp, and all in all I was pleased, relishing the thought of starting work the next day.

By the time we got back to the patio the Ruiz' were ready to leave for the next stage of the welcome festivities, so the convoy set off again, accompanied by the roar of an incoming jet thundering overhead, seemingly missing us by feet, to land just up the road. Once again I travelled with Eduardo, following the Ruiz family. This time the third person in his Renault was Irma. Pilar, Eduardo's wife, had excused herself – she had something else she had to do.

As the traffic increased, so did the kamikaze nature of Eduardo's driving, and I found myself holding on to the grip on the door. Seat-belts were unheard-of. He wove in and out of brightly painted buses packed to the seams with passengers hanging out of the windows, which had long since lost whatever glass they might once have had. The paint, I decided, was to disguise the rust. These rainbow buses hurtled down the main roads daring anyone to get in their way. From them raucous Colombian pop music was pumping out.

'They look like fun,' I said, as Eduardo did another racing gear change. 'Unless you suffer from claustrophobia.'

Irma waved her finger in front of her nose like a windscreen wiper (I didn't know then that this gesture was unique to the *paisas* to indicate something bad), and her beautiful eyes looked up to the heavens as she told me never even to think of travelling on them or I would suffer a fate worse than death. She had never been on one in her life, she said. 'They are only for the lower classes.'

Of course, this made me determined to try them out – which I did, in spite of regular accounts in the local newspaper of fatal crashes involving buses, which vied only with stories of fatal crashes involving aircraft.

The apartment building had its own underground garage and the 'watchman', as security guards were called, gave Gloria's father a smart salute. The Ruiz family lived in a high-rise apartment more for security reasons than anything else. As a rich man, Don Enrique was a prime target for kidnapping, which was endemic even then throughout Colombia. Although the Medellín Mafia ruled the kidnapping roost in the city, they weren't the only people you had to watch out for: there was the ELN, Ejército de Liberación or the Army of Liberation, and FARC, Fuerzas Armadas Revolucionarias de Colombia, or the Colombian Revolutionary Army. But, as I later found out, nowhere – and nothing – was secure: when we got out of the car Gustavo, Irma's husband, took the precaution of removing the windscreen wipers and put them out of sight.

'Surely no one would steal those,' I said. 'Especially not here.' This was, after all, a secure, guarded car park.

41

'Oh, yes, they would,' he replied.

Though Gloria's mother, Doña Matilde, had talked about 'taking tea', Don Enrique immediately got out the finest Scotch whisky – he loved the good life and I soon found myself drinking a Scotch on the rocks and looking out on a truly amazing panorama. The apartment was on the eighth floor and although it was only about half past five, it was getting towards dusk and lights were coming on all over Medellín. They looked like jewels. I thought of London and the view from my flat above the Harmsworth. The city was immense, spreading out along the plain and up into the hills – mountains, really – that surrounded it, and everywhere now twinkling with lights.

Far below, the dim hum of traffic could be heard. The wall around the balcony seemed absurdly low and I felt myself standing well back: one little push or trip and it seemed to me that you could fall into the void without any problem at all. I shivered. This was the cue for another whisky and I went inside as the temperature dropped, surprisingly suddenly.

Every now and then the maid would bring in some delicious *empanadas* – little meat-filled pasties, which I had had and enjoyed in London when I visited my Colombian friends' houses. I drifted in and out in the conversation, partly due to jet-lag but mostly because I was finding it hard to get used to this rapid-fire *paisa* accent, and as they could understand my European Spanish perfectly, they talked to me as though I was a local. That first evening I was acutely aware of how small everyone was: Gloria's father was about the same height as she was, about five feet two.

Pretty soon my head began to ache and I felt the extreme fatigue of jet-lag and prolonged concentration. Soon Eduardo came over and said that it was, perhaps, time we made a move, so we made our excuses and left. However, I was mistaken in imagining that he had seen I was fading. He was simply determined to show me the city that he loved and, leaving the Renault in the Ruiz' car park, we set off walking to what soon become one of my favourite places, the Pasaje Junin.

Every Spanish city has somewhere where people just stroll – in Barcelona it's the Ramblas. It was soon clear that this was a prosperous part of town, the *pasaje* was lined with small shops selling clothes, books and jewellery.

It was eight o'clock in the evening and the older inhabitants had largely gone home, so it was full of young people just hanging out, flirting and chattering. The first thing that struck me as unusual was that everyone looked at each other and talked to complete strangers and especially pretty girls, of which there were countless numbers.

'*Bizcocho!*'

I started at a voice close to my ear and turned to see a girl, who looked like an advertisement for a Bounty Bar, smiling at me.

'Ah-ha,' said Eduardo. 'You will have no problems here.' And he laughed. I was mystified.

'*Bizcocho* is a little cake,' he explained, 'and this means she likes you, that she would like to eat you like a little cake.'

I could see I was going to be happy.

The girl had already passed on, satisfied with getting the first strike in. It seemed that everyone was chatting everyone else up, amazing to an Englishman used to the glum fixed-to-the-pavement stares of girls at home.

We went upstairs to what would soon become my favourite bar with a bird's-eye view of the people walking up and down the Pasaje Junin. The people of Medellín had even coined a verb for this – *juninear*. All fatigue vanished as I watched the almost exclusively young stroll up and down, pretending to window-shop but in reality on the prowl for more exciting things.

Eduardo clapped his hands and I jumped. It turned out that this was the routine way of getting a waiter's attention. Two ice-cold beers appeared and I sat back again to people-watch. I was transfixed – the whole town seemed to be out and about.

Among the multitude of young people and street entertainers were beggars of all descriptions, *gamines* hawking American cigarettes, shouting what sounded like 'Kenny Molbro', Kent and Marlboro being the two brands most favoured by Colombian smokers. Contraband, Eduardo informed me, but he didn't seem to care. I would soon find out that most Colombians replaced things that were stolen by buying them back from the thieves, everything from television sets to windscreen wipers, and indeed every conceivable method of making money was on display that evening – legal and illegal. There was no social security so people had to do whatever it took. It was disconcerting to see so many beggars and the apparent indifference displayed to them by everyone else.

'They are called *pordioseros*,' Eduardo told me, as we made our way back to the car. It was a word I didn't know. 'Because they are always calling on God. Listen to them.'

And I did. '*Por Dios*,' a voice on the pavement said piteously. For God.

On our way back up the Pasaje Junin, Eduardo pointed out the tallest building in the city, a veritable skyscraper. The inhabitants of Medellín had been so amazed by it, that when they saw it they still said, '*Ave Maria, pues*' – a phrase used by *paisas* in the same way we might say 'bloody hell'. Ever since it had been known as the Ave Maria Building.

¡Viva El Vet!

I was exhausted, but I was full of excitement as to what this new life held for me. There were so many pretty girls sauntering by – and half of them giving the stranger in their midst a look that anywhere else would have been a downright invitation. I was just smiling back at one particularly beautiful girl when suddenly a *gamin* ran past and grabbed her handbag. She had been off guard for only a second, but that was all that it took.

A great shout went up that was carried on up the *pasaje* like an echo. '*Ladrón, ladrón*' – thief. A group of young men took off after the young rascal, who couldn't have been more than eight, but he disappeared up a side-street. A minute or so later they were back, empty-handed. Bag and boy had gone.

Twenty minutes later we were back at the house. Maria, the maid, was summoned out of the alcove at the back of the kitchen where she slept to provide *tintos* – not red wine, as this would mean in Spain, but black coffee. Fortunately, Colombian coffee is never very strong and within twenty minutes I was in bed asleep.

Eduardo's last words were: 'Tomorrow, eight o'clock.'

Chapter 4

At eight Eduardo was already in the office drinking the first of the innumerable *tintos* that Maria made for him during the day. Cristina, the practice nurse, was busying around, but there was no sign of any clients, not to mention animals. I decided not to tell Eduardo about the hundred or so patients a day that came through our doors at the Harmsworth.

By ten, there was still not a sign of anything or anyone. I wondered what was happening. Eduardo seemed unperturbed, deep in the local paper *El Colombiano*. Then, all of a sudden, two patients arrived at once.

The first was an English cocker spaniel, although it wouldn't have stood a chance at Crufts. Its upper jaw protruded over the lower, giving the dog a sad, rather comical look. He was called Coco and had been off-colour for ten days or so, his owner explained. This hadn't improved his temper, and he let out a howl as soon as he saw two people in green coats approaching, then bared his teeth – or at least the teeth in his upper jaw. 'Coco! Coco!' his owner said reprovingly. She was middle-aged and, judging from her clothes, rich. Later I found out she came from the Poblado district of Medellín where all the houses had their own watchmen.

Eduardo had collared many of the dog-owners in that part of town, much to the annoyance of his fellow vets, but as far as I was concerned, this was a mixed blessing: although they undoubtedly had money and seemed only too happy to part with it to keep their cherished pets in good condition, extreme ferociousness seemed to be a highly desirable characteristic of most of their dogs.

Coco was too small to be much threat to Cristina and Eduardo, however, and they sprang into action. I watched from the sidelines.

A muzzle appeared and Cristina put this deftly around the dog's mouth while Eduardo distracted him. Then bandages were tied to his feet and, with a neat bit of *kung fu*, Eduardo got the dog on his side while Cristina attached the paws to some specially made ties on the side of the table. Within one minute Coco had been immoblised and trussed up like a chicken. I had never seen anything like it. He lay there looking up at us, twitching his lips from time to time. But he was beaten and he knew it. The examination could now begin.

Rapid-fire *paisa* Spanish ensued while Eduardo pulled and prodded the spaniel's abdomen and listened to his chest. I only caught the odd word here and there and wondered what on earth the conclusions would be.

Eduardo stood up, and filled a syringe, which he plunged into Coco's skin. He pronounced the dog to be suffering from overloading of the liver – *sobrecarga hepática*. This seemed to be a common complaint, often brought on, according to my new colleague, by the owner feeding the animal all sorts of rubbish instead of proper, good-quality food.

Eduardo retired to his desk and started to hammer away at his typewriter. It seemed an age before he finished and passed me the prescription – when it comes to drugs, the language of veterinary science is Latin, as it is in human medicine. He had listed half a dozen remedies, ranging from vitamin B tablets to antibiotics and others I hadn't heard of. The clients liked to have lots of medicines, he explained later. It was the same with their own ailments. The prescription would have to be taken to the chemist, as Eduardo did not stock any drugs himself. The whole consultation took half an hour and resulted in a fee of a hundred pesos, about £1.50, which, even in those days, wasn't much. (I soon found out that a hundred pesos would buy a meal in a restaurant that would last me an entire day.) With much hand-shaking and smiling, Coco and his owner left.

Meanwhile, Cristina was squirting surgical spirit on to the table. I had just turned my back when there was a sudden *whoosh* and I turned round to see the table in flames. I hadn't heard Eduardo light a match, which he had dropped on to its surface: it was his standard method of disinfecting the all-metal table between patients. It made the whole surgery smell like a distillery but the clients didn't seem to mind. Unusual, perhaps, but effective.

Next through the consulting-room door was a Yorkshire terrier puppy of about five months old. She was called Cucky, pronounced Cooky. Her owner was another wealthy woman, who had arrived in a chauffeur-driven car. This, Eduardo informed me, via mime and a display of eye-rolling, was to be a lucrative operation, consisting of ear-cropping, tail-docking and vaccine thrown in. Three hundred pesos in all.

I watched with increasing dismay as the operation began. First Cucky was tied up as the spaniel had been, although she capitulated right away. Next she was given an anaesthetic into the vein. A quick swab of the ears and Eduardo showed me how to measure where to cut them, then sliced off half of each ear with scissors. He cauterised any bleeding vessels with a little hand-held instrument. The ear was stitched up with a continuous stitch which I had to admit was deftly done. Finally the tail was amputated near to the base and a couple of stitches put in.

Half an hour later Cucky was coming round with a low moan that made my heart bleed. The purpose of all this was purely fashion: most dogs owned by wealthy people, even dogs of dubious pedigree, had their ears cropped and their tails cut off. Breeders and owners alike admired the prick-ear effect and it seemed that a veterinary surgeon's reputation could be made or broken on this one operation. I noticed that Eduardo took great care getting the cut just right and bandaged the ears afterwards to ensure that they stayed upright.

I muttered that ear-cropping was illegal in England and said I would have to see many more done if I were ever to try it myself. Privately I thought I would rather starve. Later there were days when I literally did go without food when I was away from the clinic but I never sacrificed my principles on ear-cropping. Not that starvation was likely to afflict Eduardo, who seemed to have an inexhaustible supply of food and drink, particularly *aguardiente*.

There were no further clients during the morning, and at two o'clock we retired next door for lunch, which as always had been prepared by Maria the maid, though being classed as the lowest of the low, she didn't eat with us but ate on her own at the back of the kitchen.

The food was quite plain, with meat and salad the staple. There were no spices or garlic and it was a million miles away from the Spanish food I had been eating only a few weeks previously. Eduardo had been expecting me to suffer from traveller's tummy and was impressed by the way I had prepared myself before my arrival, with lots of meals out, home cooking from Gloria and my journey round Spain.

However, the most unusual thing to me about that first lunch was that it was accompanied by milk – nobody, it seemed, drank wine with their meals in Medellín. It was beer, *aguardiente* or milk. My Colombian friends in London had definitely dispensed with that tradition.

The sweet was something called a *bocadillo* with *quesito*. I knew that in Spain *bocadillo* meant a sandwich and *quesito* meant a small cheese. However, this *bocadillo* turned out to be a kind of guava jelly, and the cheese was soft and bland. It made for a delicious combination though. Half-way through the meal there was a knock at the door. Eduardo glanced through the window and shouted, '*No hay nada!*' There is nothing here.

I caught a glimpse of a disconsolate figure shuffling away. Eduardo had by now settled down with his newspaper and an *aguardiente*. 'What was that about?' I asked, curious to know how he had decided not even to open the door.

'Some *pordiosero*,' he replied, yawning. 'We get a lot of them round here.' There were two further interruptions of the same ilk over the two-hour lunch break.

Later Maria told me that you always had to ensure that there was someone in the house at all times – an important role of the maid. If not, you were sure to be burgled: the word would go out within hours that the house was empty. As a result she hardly ever set foot outside. If Eduardo's wife, Pilar, wasn't available to do the shopping then Maria would do it, but only if one of us was around. In an emergency she would get one of her relatives to house-sit while she went out. To leave the house unoccupied was a sackable offence.

At three we went back into the clinic, where Cristina had been bustling about during our absence. It seemed she didn't get a paid lunch break.

¡Viva El Vet!

I was in for a shock when the next client arrived: a young, excitable woman with another Yorkshire terrier.

The shock was that Eduardo had nipped out to buy another bottle of his favourite tipple and I had to deal with anything that came in. It took me back to my first consultation in Canterbury: I had gulped when I was told to go into Room Four and get on with it. At least my first client there had spoken English. With my heart thumping, I attempted to get a history, the first step in any diagnosis.

My basic questioning unleashed a truly amazing torrent of Medellín-style Spanish. The main problem for me – apart from the speed – was that every word was used in the diminutive, so that teeth became 'little teeth', nose 'little nose' and so on. Fortunately Cristina was at hand. Although she didn't speak English, she quickly became adept at translating *paisa* Spanish into a slow, simple Spanish that I could understand.

This time I affected a learned air then retired with Cristina for a translation.

The little Yorkshire terrier was a veteran for Colombia – nearly nine years old. There was a thriving trade in stolen pedigree dogs and owners had to guard their pets with their lives. Up and down the Pasaje Junin you could find various ne'er-do-wells with shivering specimens on string leads hissing, '*Se vende*' – for sale! It appeared that the Yorkie was losing his front teeth and constantly rubbing his nose. When I went back in to examine him, I saw that one tooth at the front was practically hanging out and the others weren't much better. Given the state he was in, it didn't surprise me to learn that he wasn't eating. Serious dental work was the only answer, I informed the owner.

This produced hysteria with floods of tears because the woman was convinced that her pet would never survive an anaesthetic.

Cristina began to get out the instruments and told the owner she could wait outside while we did it. Cristina knew only too well that we had to strike while the iron was hot or we wouldn't get another chance: it was common for owners to get four or five opinions before consenting to treatment and I was soon to get used to giving third and fourth opinions on patients that had done the rounds.

Cristina was amazed that I didn't truss our patient up. A quick jab into the vein and he was unconscious. On closer inspection I realised that half of his teeth had to come out. One piece of good news was that Eduardo's collection of dental instruments was much better than I had expected. In fact, dentistry was something the *paisas* excelled at: there was a thriving dental school in Medellín and lots of dentists, all making a reasonable living. Young people took great care of their appearance – the rich ones anyway – and most people seemed to have perfect teeth.

Twenty minutes later a groggy Yorkie was waking up, apparently none the worse for his experience. Eduardo walked in, carrying four bottles of *aguardiente*, just as the ecstatically grateful client walked out with her pet under her arm, his tongue lolling out of the side of his mouth but very much alive and already feeling better.

But the good news, as far as Eduardo was concerned, was that the clinic was three hundred pesos better off and our reputation would benefit, which would mean more rich clients and more pesos. Cause for celebration. A glass of *aguardiente* duly appeared alongside a glass of water. There were two ways of drinking *aguardiente*: the first was to pour water into it and drink the cloudy mixture. This was the boys' way. The men's way was to down it in one then take a sip of water.

'Salud!' said Eduardo, downing his in one. Determined not to be considered a girl's blouse at this stage in our relationship, I did the same. However, discretion proved the better part of valour and I decided to draw the line at one. 'There may be more patients,' I pointed out, but Eduardo did not think so. It was nearing six o'clock. Here, near the equator, nightfall was around six all year round. No clients would venture out now. Medellín became a dangerous place after dark and I was warned repeatedly not to walk about at night. Advice that, with the arrogance of youth, I was destined to ignore.

Living above the shop had its disadvantages. After dinner with Eduardo the phone rang. A dog had been shot by the watchman in an apartment block but was still alive. The caller wasn't a client of the clinic and Eduardo advised them to go somewhere else. He wasn't going to get involved with shootings, he explained, even though he always carried his Beretta around with him. It seemed, just like in America, that everyone had a gun in the house. I shivered at the thought of it and turned in early, exhausted by my day. There had been few clients but my huge efforts to understand and make myself understood had been wearing. From O level Spanish I was going to be on a steep learning curve.

The next morning I was brushing my teeth when I heard the sound of gun fire. With Eduardo's words of the previous night in my ears I hurried downstairs. Tentatively I opened the lounge door and there, on the patio, was Eduardo at target practice. Well, that was what he called it but, frankly, he didn't seem to be firing at anything, more letting off steam. He stopped when I arrived, but his Beretta became a regular alarm call over the next few weeks.

David Grant

Breakfast consisted of coffee – Eduardo was amazed that I had it white with no sugar – and *arepas*, a kind of cake made of maize. A bit of an acquired taste this but I soon got to like them. As he downed his third *tinto* of the morning, Eduardo said that while he was still around I should get my work visa sorted out. What did he mean, *while he was still around*?

He waved his hands noncommittaly. He was planning a trip out of town in a couple of weeks' time. I had already proved I was capable and the practice didn't need both of us to be there at the same time. And I had to admit it was true: there wasn't enough work to sustain one vet, let alone two. But the idea of being on my own was more than a little alarming. 'Don't worry,' he said, reading my thoughts. 'Remember, you will have Cristina with you.'

Before I had left England Gloria had assured me that getting a work visa would be simple once I was in Colombia; it would need only a few words in the right ear from my *palanca*, her father, Don Enrique Ruiz. However, by some stroke of ill luck the position in relation to visas had undergone a radical change the week before I arrived. The country was apparently being inundated with foreigners – mainly American hippies – in search of Colombian marijuana, which was viewed as the champagne of the dope-smoking fraternity. They would come in on a tourist visa, just as I had, then change it for a working visa, which allowed them to teach English or take whatever work they could find and, more importantly, to stay pretty much unsupervised for a year. As these people contributed nothing to the economy, someone in the government had decided to make it difficult for gringos to get a work visa.

Now you had to have a medical, a blood test, a chest X-ray – none of which came cheap – and the final sting in the tail was that the visa could only be applied for from a foreign country, the nearest being Venezuela. To make it even more expensive, the visa had to be collected in person in the country where it had been processed: I would have to make two trips to Venezuela.

Before I could begin the process the local veterinary college had to approve my qualifications, and I began to envisage an early return home: compared with the ornate certificates that adorned the walls of Eduardo's clinic, resplendent with stamps and gold lettering, my degree from the Royal Veterinary College came a very poor second.

A few evenings later I accompanied Eduardo to a meeting of the local veterinary big-wigs where they inspected this sad-looking piece of paper while he made a speech on my behalf, saying how well qualified and what a good surgeon I was. Which was interesting, given that at that point he had seen me wield nothing more lethal than a syringe of anaesthetic. However, it seemed that the president was an Anglophile because my credentials were approved and my right to work was rubber-stamped in about five minutes. Eduardo and I celebrated with a beer in the Pasaje Junin.

A few days before I had booked my flight for Venezuela Eduardo poked his head round the door and with a cheery wave said he would see us after lunch. As we had no potential customers I sat down to puzzle my way through *El Colombiano* while Cristina set about updating some of the clinic records.

Cristina had worked with Eduardo since he had started the clinic about ten years before, and knew all the clients personally, especially the few foreigners, who were mainly German and American. Eduardo had already cornered this market and one of his aims in having me around was that I would expand it. Although Cristina's family were desperately poor – she lived with her mother in a nearby flat – and she herself had left school at fourteen, Cristina was highly intelligent and spoke a clear, seemingly educated Spanish. She had no difficulty in understanding me or, more importantly, in translating into simple Spanish the sometimes complex histories of our patients. On one occasion, though, even she could not stop me making a complete fool of myself. It was about half an hour after Eduardo had disappeared on yet another of his mysterious absences when I was confronted with a slobbering old boxer dog, Pepe.

At first glance Pepe had merely looked strange, with his obligatory cropped ears and hangdog expression, but a quick examination showed him to be very sick indeed. His temperature hardly registered and his pulse was very weak. He had been brought down from the hills around Medellín by the *mayordomo* – the farm manager of a large coffee plantation in a village in the mountains. He had eaten '*choclo*', the *mayordomo* said. He was in severe pain – no doubt about that – with a tense abdomen. But chocolate? I couldn't understand it.

'What kind of chocolate?' I asked.

Suddenly both Cristina and the *mayordomo*, Alejandro, burst out laughing. Not chocolate, *choclo*. They tried to explain what this was, but even Cristina failed to make me understand – it didn't help that she couldn't stop laughing. I was totally at a loss. In the end I looked it up in the dictionary. Corn-on-the-cob.

Now I understood why the dog was so ill. I sedated him, and when I examined his abdomen I could feel a lump in the intestines. He'd eaten it whole and it was stuck. Cristina explained that the dog had been to see another vet who had diagnosed the problem correctly but advised putting

Pepe down. His verdict was that at ten years of age Pepe wouldn't survive the operation.

The owner had instructed his *mayordomo* to bring Pepe to us for a second opinion. He had heard about the *inglés* who might be able to perform a miracle and he was reluctant to accept the death sentence for his six-year-old daughter's favourite pet.

It would be the first time I had performed surgery on a dog without intravenous fluids and an anaesthetic machine, but I decided to give it a try. Pepe would either survive or not. It would have to be quick, basic surgery and I would have to do it with Cristina. Alejandro opted to watch.

Five minutes later Pepe was slumbering on the operating table and I was incising into his abdomen. Quite soon a red, angry-looking intestine popped into view. Another cut and out came the corn-on-the-cob, to the amusement of Alejandro

'Eh! *Ave Maria, pues.*' He whistled – got out a cloth and wrapped the corn-on-the-cob in it to take home. The most expensive *choclo* in Colombia, was how he put it. Twenty minutes later Pepe was coming round. Colombian vets believed in recovery in the home and not at the clinic: at the Harmsworth Pepe would have been in for three days minimum and I saw the semi-conscious dog leave with reservations. Cristina, though, was delighted – she had never seen that operation before and was full of it for the rest of the day. Eduardo, too, was delighted when he heard the news. My reputation was now assured, he told me.

With some of the proceeds in my pocket I decided to go into town and eat in the Pasaje Junin that evening. Against everyone's advice I decided to catch the bus, having taken the precaution of putting my watch into my pocket. On the surface I didn't look any richer than the other passengers,

I decided. The group waiting around the bus stop included lots of Indian women in traditional long dresses, carrying fruit for sale, and there were also the ubiquitous *gamines*.

Suddenly there was a commotion. Just as the bus arrived a woman in front of me, who I later discovered had her fare of two pesos in her hand, screamed suddenly as the grubby banknote was snatched out of her hand by one of the urchins – even the equivalent of a penny was to be found in note form and became unimaginably dirty yet stayed in circulation, only to be stolen by desperate starving children. When I recounted the story to Eduardo he dismissed my English-liberal concern with a wave of his hand. He regarded them simply as *mala gente* – bad people.

We were well and truly crammed in, literally hanging out of the windows. A sign inside clearly said maximum number of passengers 40. We were at least seventy. At each stop the bus took off as though we were in a Grand Prix, and we swayed about as it avoided the many potholes, accompanied by the latest, frantic and very loud salsa number. The passengers seemed confident in the driver's ability to get us there and enjoyed the music. The bus didn't have a back door and every now and then an illegal passenger would join us – the driver had no way of knowing when this happened since there were no mirrors on the bus. In fact, he relied on the goodwill of passengers at the back to let him know when he could leave each stop. The journey took about fifteen minutes and I was crammed in the middle with no chance of escape if there had been a crash. At thirty, the possibility didn't cross my mind, and I was more interested in holding on to my wallet and watch. Pickpockets abounded on buses.

When I got off I quickly found the bar to which Eduardo had taken me on my first night. Feeling rather embarrassed

¡Viva El Vet!

I clapped my hands loudly, just as Eduardo had to get their attention, but no one seemed to find it odd and I soon had an ice-cold beer and a huge bowl of bean stew in front of me, swiftly followed by a salad. To English sensibilities it seemed rude but in fact it was a very sensible solution – none of that business about catching the waiter's eye. For the first time since I had arrived I felt at home. In fact, I was in seventh heaven. I had a panoramic view of the goings-on below and watched the young people threading their way along the *pasaje*, gossiping, confiding, teasing, flirting.

My evening was only marred by a nagging worry about Pepe. I would rather have kept him in. I had arranged for Alejandro to phone the next morning to tell me how he was, and I went to bed in good time ready for an early start.

At eight next morning I was startled to see Alejandro and a sick-looking Pepe in the back of a pick-up truck. Apparently, as soon as the dog had come round he had staggered into the kitchen, helped himself to another corn-on-the-cob and gulped it down before anyone could stop him. The whole saga had to be repeated but this time I insisted on keeping him in for the night and Cristina begged an intravenous giving-set and bag of fluid from the local children's hospital so that I could prevent him becoming dehydrated. It meant staying up late with the dog and missing out on a party organised by Gloria's family – but I was going to get that dog right, whatever it took.

Chapter 5

Later that evening Eduardo came in rather drunk and pronounced that the dog would live. He was already believing his own myth that the *inglés* could work miracles.

I was due to go to Venezuela in two days' time and, over two *tintos*, he gave me all the advice I needed to cross the border when I arrived. The cheapest way would be to fly to Cúcuta on the Colombian side of the border, then take a bus to San Antonio, the Venezuelan border town, because a taxi would be too expensive. The warnings came thick and fast. The bus station was overrun with thieves and conmen, he said. I had to hand my money only to the driver. I had to tell the driver I would need to stop at the border to get my passport stamped. And I had to be careful with my passport and never let it out of my sight. He also gave me the name of a hotel in case I needed to stay the night. The changes in the visa regulations would ensure even longer queues than usual, he warned.

Pepe staggered in to join us at about two in the morning and jumped up on the sofa beside Eduardo, who had already nodded off. I left them to it and reflected that we could truthfully say that the vets had stayed up all night with the dog to see that he was all right.

During those early weeks I had been helping Eduardo and getting to know the clients. Much of the work, as at home, was routine, with the occasional fascinating case that

¡Viva El Vet!

I would never have seen in England. The day before I was due to go to Venezuela one such turned up.

The owner, a wealthy German called Heinrich Schmidt, brought in a giant German shepherd called Fritz. Herr Schmidt had been in Colombia since the end of the Second World War and was a bit vague about why he had come. This was an occasion, I decided, when it was better not to ask. Whatever his history, he was now doing well for himself: he owned several banana plantations and lived in a mansion on the edge of Medellín with his Colombian wife and six children.

He spoke excellent if heavily accented English and explained that his dog, employed to guard the family concern, had developed several large swellings on his ears and face. After Eduardo and Cristina had trussed Fritz up in their usual way, Eduardo suggested I examine the lumps. They seemed quite large and fleshy with a small hole in the middle. Eduardo looked on with scarcely contained glee while he watched me try to puzzle out what the lumps were. Meanwhile, Cristina was preparing some instruments for an operation: she had evidently seen this before.

'This, of course, is a Colombian disease,' I said to the owner.

Eduardo decided to let me off the hook. 'Yes,' he said. '*Gusanos*.'

Gusanos? I tried desperately to remember what that meant – worms, grubs, maggots were the words that came to mind.

While I was puzzling, Cristina swabbed each lump with surgical spirit. Then Eduardo appeared with a small pair of scissors and some forceps. Fritz had been immobilised and a large muzzle slapped on him, which evidently meant that an anaesthetic wouldn't be necessary. So it proved to be. Eduardo simply enlarged the holes and pulled a large maggot from each swelling. The hole was a breathing pore for the parasite, whatever it was. Ten minutes later, five fat maggots were lying on the operating table and a complete cure had been effected. The sight of those fleshy maggots being extracted from the holes in the dog's skin is something I will never forget.

Somehow or other I received equal credit for Fritz's return to health, for his owner told me I would receive an invitation to the Schmidt *finca* – their country farm residence – when I got back from Venezuela.

After dog and owner had been reunited, Eduardo put me out of my misery and told me that the parasite was *Cuterebra maculata*. He was obviously proud that he could conjure up its Latin name without having to go to a parasitology book. Nevertheless, that evening I looked it up myself in one of his many books. Just like me he hadn't thrown away any of the library he'd built up when he was a student and had a fine collection, mostly in English.

Cuterebra turned out to be a fly that laid its eggs near the burrows of rodents where they developed to an intermediate stage. Then a complicated migration took place to the tissues of the host, ending up with the maggots in the skin. These developed into flies, which hatched out of the skin and flew away. Occasionally dogs and cats while out hunting became the unfortunate accidental hosts. Eduardo warned me to be careful not to crush the maggots when extracting. In his early days he had seen some nasty reactions when a few dogs had died of an allergy to them after that had happened.

The next day I made my way to the airport. I was flying with a company called Aeropesca and the first sight of the aircraft sitting on the Tarmac did not inspire confidence. I had never felt entirely comfortable in the air and references to plane crashes in *El Colombiano* struck me as disproportionately frequent – second only to bus crashes. In fact the paper might have been better named *El Desastre*.

It was a propeller aircraft painted a garish blue with yellow flowers. My apprehension eased a little as we boarded and I saw that it was a Viscount, and therefore British built: all the signs were in English, if a bit faded. However, there was nothing familiar about the rest of the experience. The usual safety chat was dispensed with, and once our motley band of passengers were on board, the captain started up the engines and we were off.

Cúcuta, the border town to Venezuela, lay on the other side of the mountains and although we gained altitude rapidly we never seemed more than a few hundred feet from the ground. Soon the fields that surrounded Medellín – a surprising riot of colour – gave way to Swiss-style scenery and I could make out fields, tracks and homesteads. After ten minutes or so, we ended our ascent and headed east. In the distance I could make out specks of towns – one or two quite big. One, I suspected, was Bucaramanga, Henry Garcia's home town. I knew from the map that our flight path took us quite near it.

Eduardo had told me to look for the buses that went to San Antonio and I soon found one. It looked a bit ramshackle but it said San Antonio on the front, so who was I to ask questions? I paid a few pesos to the driver for the fare, as instructed, and got in.

But ask questions was exactly what I should have done. I was soon joined by what looked like an entire village plus their animals. There were Indian women in bowler hats and ponchos and an assorted collection of chickens, a goat and some piglets, which were allowed to roam free as we set off.

My neighbour, an impassive old lady with few teeth, nodded to me as she sat down. With my jacket, collar and tie – chosen to impress upon the consul that I was a respectable person worthy of a work visa – I stuck out like a sore thumb.

As soon as we left the town the bus turned on to a rough side-road, but it was only when it began to stop at every nook and cranny that I suspected something was wrong. Trying to communicate with the driver was difficult, and with the person I was sitting next to impossible – her own first language, I surmised, was probably not even Spanish. Eventually it dawned on me what was happening. Although I had no doubt that the bus would eventually wind up at the border – after all, it had said San Antonio clearly on the front – it was market day and all the villagers were going to the border too. I was right. The journey took two hours. In a taxi it would have taken twenty minutes. After crossing the border I arrived at the Colombian consulate in San Antonio at four o'clock, an hour before it closed.

San Antonio was not a big place. Across the way from the consulate there were a couple of basic hotels, though no sign of the one that Eduardo had mentioned, and by now I knew I was going to need one. The flight back was scheduled for six p.m. but it was soon obvious that I would never make that: there were six people in front of me and the queue – if such it could be called – hadn't moved since I arrived.

I decided to forget it for now and return early the next morning – even Venezuelan red tape couldn't take all day, I decided. I checked into the nearest hotel and had a tepid shower before venturing out. Even though there was only about an hour to go before sunset, it was still uncomfortably hot: it was only four hundred feet above sea level compared with Medellín's five thousand.

¡Viva El Vet!

My first impression of Venezuela was that there seemed to be more money about than there was in Colombia. The cars – mostly American and a few Renaults – were in reasonably good condition, which meant that there was tread on the tyres, unlike in Medellín where everybody drove on bald ones.

The local beer was good and cold and I managed to get a meal without too much molesting from beggars. However, when I was drinking my coffee a shoe-black arrived and started tut-tutting about the state of my shoes. We haggled a bit about the price and then he set about restoring my brown shoes to something like respectability.

'*Americano*?' he asked me.

'No. English,' I replied, but this made no difference. He automatically thought England was part of the USA. I was a gringo. It was impossible to guess his age, presumably in his teens or twenties, but his face was burned deep brown by the relentless sun. I turned down his offer to introduce me to his sister.

'OK, Doctor,' he said. Everything he said to me ended 'Doctor.' Eventually I asked him how he knew I was a doctor. 'In this country any son-of-a-bitch is a doctor.' I left him laughing at his own joke and wandered off back to the hotel.

As the fan in my room didn't work I settled for another tepid shower and lay down on the bed looking at the blood-stained walls – a mosquito graveyard. There was a basic mosquito net hanging from the ceiling tied in a loose knot. When I untied it to fit round the bed it was full of holes. I had a choice: to shut the windows and suffocate or leave them open and be bitten to death. I immediately turned off the light and hoped they would just go away. There was no problem with mosquitoes in Medellín: it was too high.

I tried to sleep, but for a long time the whine of a single mosquito kept me awake. I wanted to be back in Medellín at the clinic, which was already feeling like home. Eventually, in spite of a solitary cockroach that scuttled across the sheets, sleep came. I woke early, showered, dressed, paid my bill and had breakfast within sight of the Consulate.

Even though I was there early five people had beaten me to it and I was beginning to panic, anticipating another night in this tropical 'paradise'. Eventually after much scrutiny of my documents by a succession of officials, who all looked as if they might have had parts in *Our Man In Havana*, I was told that everything was in order and that I would be notified when my visa was ready. I would have to come back then to pick it up. This seemed a ridiculously long-winded way of going about things but I had no doubt it dramatically slowed the number of gringo hippies getting into the country, as it was intended to.

I walked out, relieved, and started looking for a taxi: there was no way I was going to repeat the ridiculous bus journey and, anyway, I had only an hour and a half to get to the airport for the next plane back. One of the other visa applicants, standing on what passed for a pavement outside the Consulate, read my mind. 'You looking for a taxi?' he said.

He was a clean-shaven and well dressed – collar, tie, young man about my age.

'You American?' I asked.

'Sure am!' We shook hands. 'Chuck. And this is my wife Socorro.'

A woman emerged from the shade of the Consulate door looking sulky. Socorro was obviously Latin-American, not only because of her looks but her name, which literally meant 'help'. I have since met several Socorros and wondered why they were given such an odd-sounding name, at least to English ears.

They had just got married, Chuck explained, and were going back to Medellín to live. A taxi appeared and the newlyweds' luggage was loaded in. Fortunately all I had brought with me was a hold-all, which I held on my lap. With a lurch and a flurry of dust, we set off to the airport. Socorro looked moodily out of the window while her husband did all the talking. 'Do you mind if I ask you something, Dave?'

'No,' I replied warily.

'Do you believe in God the Father and Jesus, His Son?'

I had no time to reply because Chuck launched himself into a passionate sermon on the need to repent and be saved.

The sermon hadn't gone unnoticed by the taxi driver. He slowed down as if listening to the monologue then took a right and moved down the back-streets. I glanced at the meter – it was clicking away at an alarming rate. Twenty minutes had gone and we should have been in sight of the airport by now. I tried to ask our driver how much longer we would be but was drowned out by Chuck, his eyes ablaze with religious zeal. The meter was registering some preposterous sum for what should have been a fifteen-minute journey but eventually the whine of a jet signified our proximity to the airport. First, though, we had to go through the border control. This time, mercifully, we were waved through and the taxi deposited us in front of the terminal not long after.

I jumped out and paid half the fare. It was only just over ten minutes to departure time. The check-in lady looked doubtful, but with only hand luggage and a beseeching smile I was allowed through. Now I understood why latecomers for flights are called runners.

David Grant

I made it just in time to board the last bus, which took us to the Viscount waiting on the runway. As the bus stuttered into life I could see Chuck in a heated argument with a woman who had a 'sour milk' face, a phrase often used of miserable-looking people both in Spain and Colombia.

It was obvious they weren't going to catch this flight, with all their luggage. Socorro looked on sullenly as Chuck lost his rag. No milk of human kindness there. Once on board I slumped in my seat, sweating profusely. The stewardess, taking pity on me, served me with an orange juice and we took off exactly on time.

I sat back in my window seat and heaved a sigh of relief. But it seemed our adventures weren't over yet. Instead of the usual routine climb after take-off, I realised we were doing swoops low over the undulating hills. At first I thought something terrible had happened – after all, they always say that taking off and landing are the most dangerous times in a flight. On looking out of my window I could see the occasional *campesino* waving at us, quite unperturbed. This went on for twenty minutes before suddenly as if on a whim, the plane went into a steep climb and headed west. A few minutes later the captain explained in English that we had been looking for a crashed plane.

He didn't bother to repeat his announcement in Spanish so I assumed that it had been made for my benefit – as far as I could judge I was the only gringo aboard since Chuck hadn't made it. For the locals it must have been a common occurrence: there were no more than twenty passengers and they seemed to have taken the swoops and low-flying stunts as par for the course. With a tail wind we made reasonable time and, in spite of the twenty-minute scenic detour, we flew into Medellín only ten minutes late. As we landed there was a ripple of applause, whether in thanks for a safe landing or simply arriving I wasn't sure. It was a warmer night than usual, shirtsleeve weather, and I was surprised to see the corpulent figure of Eduardo waiting for me in the arrivals lounge.

We jumped into his ageing Renault and headed off towards the Medellín football club stadium, which wasn't far from the clinic. He had some important news for me and wanted to talk about it over dinner. In the meantime I wanted to know about Pepe. Was he all right? Yes, apparently there had been no repetition of the corn-on-the-cob incident and the youngest daughter had spent her entire time checking that none had been left around.

We weren't eating in the stadium building, but the area boasted a number of restaurants where you could eat outside and Eduardo had reserved a table. I was glad to be 'home': the heat in Venezuela had reminded me of just how perfect Medellín was. When I had a couple of beers inside me and was tucking into fried chicken and salad, Eduardo, looking more morose than usual, began to tell me of his plans.

It seemed that things between him and Pilar were not good and that they were going to separate. He was looking at a job in Apartado, several hundred miles in the north, in the jungle, miles from anywhere. Pilar had 'un amigo', he explained, as he fingered the Beretta in its holster, and their marriage was as good as dead. Although it came as a shock, I can't say that it altogether surprised me. I had hardly seen Eduardo's wife since I arrived.

Now that the documents to get a working visa were a formality, Eduardo continued, he felt I could run things while he found somewhere to live. He would be back in a week or two to sort things out. How did I feel about that?

'When are you going?' I asked, still trying to take it all in.

'Tomorrow at three. There's an airline called Aces, which flies a dozen people there once a week. It's a very small plane and I got the last seat, otherwise I would have had to wait another week. And I just don't think I can go on that long. Things are not good.'

At this point I thought he would burst into tears so I quickly called for a bottle of *aguardiente*, the only thing more or less guaranteed to cheer him up.

'So from tomorrow, David, you'll be on your own. But I have every confidence in you. I've signed thirty prescriptions and Cristina can type in whatever drugs you need – she knows everything.' Another pause before he added, 'I'm going to miss her,' and took a large swig at the thought.

During the meal I had noticed a couple of children looking fixedly at our plates, which contained scraps of food. One caught my eye and I raised an eyebrow. He took this as permission and in a flash the children swooped on our plates and swallowed the remains in seconds. They ran off as the waiter cursed them and their mothers.

'*Lameplatos*,' said Eduardo – plate-lickers: yet another variant to add to my list of specialist beggars. I was reminded once again that in Colombia you had to fend for yourself – there was no welfare state. Tomorrow I, too, would be fending for myself. I blanched at the prospect. Before I had time to start worrying a group of musicians approached us. For ten pesos they would play any tune.

Eduardo, by now feeling expansive with the better part of the bottle of *aguardiente* inside him, requested '*Pueblito Viejo*' – 'Little Old Village'. I had already heard this song at Colombian get-togethers in London. It was about as sentimental as you could get, and talked of returning to die in the village where you had grown up and learned to love before finding out what sadness and ingratitude that could bring. For a group charging only ten pesos, less than 20p, they played beautifully with astounding guitar work. It was magical to be serenaded in the warm night, and the words suited Eduardo's mood.

'*Pueblito viejo*,' he said, gesturing towards the centre of Medellín a few miles away, and sighed. We paid the bill and he staggered to the car, not objecting when I suggested that I drive the short distance to the clinic.

The next day I woke bright and early. For a moment I couldn't think why, then I remembered. Although Eduardo's plane didn't leave until the afternoon, I was now in charge. Technically I was working illegally. Anyone could help a vet – Cristina was an example – but issuing prescriptions was something only a registered veterinarian could do, which was why Eduardo had signed a padful. However, Eduardo didn't seem to think it was a problem: I had jumped through all the hoops to get my work visa and it was only a question of waiting for the paperwork to come through. And his needs were pressing: he wanted to sort out his new life.

As I was showering, I realised with a start that this was the first time since qualification that I was totally responsible for myself. If I didn't have any clients I wouldn't eat without dipping into my meagre savings. Until now I had always had the security of a monthly pay cheque to look forward to, come what may. This was a new experience.

A hoot announced the arrival of the first client. Out in the driveway a jeep had appeared and a Wild West character swung out of it cradling a puppy in his arms. With longish hair under a straw hat, a wide smile showing a couple of gold teeth, Pedro Ramirez swept into the clinic. He extended his hand, showing the palm before shaking hands. This was an odd affectation, which seemed rife among youngish men. It seemed to say, 'Look, I'm unarmed, it's safe to shake hands. I can't shoot you or stab you.'

From the moment he got in Pedro was all talk. He had heard about the *inglés* and wanted his puppy, Sasha, checked over. It was yet another Yorkshire terrier – he pronounced it Yor-sheer – and it was time for vaccination, ear-cropping and docking. He had travelled quite a long distance, he said, and he wanted it done today and at a special price. When he mentioned the special price he narrowed his eyes cunningly and tapped the side of his nose.

At this point Cristina came in. 'Vaccine one hundred pesos, the tail two hundred, and the tail and the ears together five hundred. But Dr David does not do the tails or the ears. Dr Serrano will do this in two weeks with the second vaccination.'

'Eh, *ave Maria, pues*. I have come a long way. I have to return?'

Cristina patiently explained that all dogs had to have two vaccinations.

'Fifty for the vaccine. And because I didn't know' – here he adopted what he clearly thought was a conciliatory tone – 'and you should have told me, three hundred for everything. Fifty now,' and at this point he got out a wad of ten-peso notes, 'and the rest in two weeks.'

Cristina made a clucking noise and wagged her finger from side to side signalling her disagreement. Watching the two of them was like watching a mime show.

'A hundred now, four hundred next time.'

A look of intense pain came across Pedro's face. His eyes rolled upwards and then he shut them as he contemplated his next move. With both hands raised as though in prayer he said, 'Seventy-five now is my final offer.'

I had visions of not eating that day. Suddenly I did

something I had never done before: I started bargaining. Inwardly I felt affronted that a client should dare to try to knock me down, but hunger had changed my perceptions.

'Ninety today,' I said, 'and I will recommend, in your particular case, a reduction of ten per cent to compensate for the journey.'

Pedro looked from side to side as though searching for an imaginary accomplice. 'Ten per cent? Make it fifteen per cent and we have a deal.' As if to emphasise his honesty he extended his hand again, showing his knife-free palm.

I shook it. 'You have a deal.'

'*Antioqueños*,' said Cristina afterwards. 'They always like to bargain. He thought you would give in as you are English.'

'What will Eduardo say?' I wondered

'He won't interfere,' she replied. 'He just wants to get away from the *bruja*' – the witch. She crossed herself at the thought of Pilar, who was supposed to dabble in witchcraft.

A few days later my fears about starving had dissipated. I was averaging four clients a day, which meant I had enough money to pay Cristina and ensure that I ate one good meal with some money left over for household expenses. I was becoming rather irritated by Pilar's habit of making private phone calls on the practice phone. After all, now Eduardo had gone, I was presumably going to have to pay for them. However, it usually happened when I was in the consulting room with a client so accosting her wasn't really an option.

One day I was reading *El Colombiano* and having a quick *tinto* when Pilar came in and picked up the phone. It was the first time I had seen her since Eduardo's dramatic announcement. This afternoon she was dressed even more provocatively than usual. She had good legs and showed them off to advantage under a skirt that barely covered the essentials. Over that she was wearing a blouse that plunged about as far as it could without giving rise to pneumonia. Her hair was up, showing off a pair of complicated gold earrings. As usual, her makeup would have done credit to a chorus girl. As she dialled the number she glared at me, then turned her back. I went next door to the operating area of the clinic where I found Cristina crossing herself and shaking her wrist in yet another typical gesture of those parts: it meant extreme excitement or, in this case, worry-worry.

'She's phoning Hector,' she hissed.

'Her boyfriend, you mean?'

'*El mafioso*.'

From the other room we could hear murmurings of endearment, which only increased Cristina's anger. She was fiercely loyal to her boss.

Although I had heard the name Hector before, I hadn't realised until now that he was Pilar's '*amigo*'. In fact, until a few days ago, I hadn't realised she had '*un amigo*'. As for Cristina's quietly muttered '*el mafioso*', I knew I would have to wait to find out what that meant because just then the bell went and another client appeared. I heard the phone click.

The patient was a female German shepherd. She had her ears back and the slightly slanted eyes that I had come to associate with a shifty temperament. She was straining at the leash and whining constantly – making it quite clear that she would rather be somewhere else.

With Cristina's help I went through the history. The owners were a rich young couple who had brought the dog from the United States. She was supposed to be a guard dog but had been off-colour ever since arrival. The wife got quite excitable detailing all the treatments and diagnoses the dog had had. I was to give the fourth opinion.

There had been more or less constant diarrhoea for the last six months and the diagnoses had been variously liver disease, enteritis, colitis and cancer. None of the various treatments had worked. The dog's name was Fanny and the last bit of helpful information was that she was a bit '*grosera*'. In the depths of my mind I struggled to find the exact English meaning of that word. 'Ugly' sprang to mind – perhaps because that was the most accurate description of Fanny, who would hardly have managed to enter Crufts. Maybe on reflection I was confusing the word with the German *grausam*, which did mean ugly. I resolved to look it up in the dictionary later.

With my best newly acquired Colombian bedside manner I said that Fanny didn't look '*grosera*' to me. I stood up and suggested we take a look on the operating table. At that moment Fanny broke free, charged across the room and took a great snap at my groin then leaped back satisfied. A great shriek went up from her owner and I sat down in excruciating pain with the room spinning in front of me. I looked down and saw blood seeping through my trousers. 'Excuse me,' I said, and staggered out to the bathroom to survey the damage.

I was in so much pain that I didn't know what to expect. Gingerly, and with great trepidation, I removed my trousers and winced. There was a gash right at the top of my leg, which had missed a more vital organ by a few centimetres.

I called for Cristina who, totally unabashed, dressed the wound with the help of lint and sticking plaster. While she was deftly pushing the jagged edges together I reached out and pulled a dictionary from the shelf above the desk. I looked up *grosera* in my dictionary. It meant bad-mannered.

Bad-mannered? Psychopathic, more like. Meanwhile, in the confusion Fanny and her owners had disappeared. I could have cried – all this pain and no money. And then a dreadful afterthought. What about rabies?

Cristina assured me that rabies didn't exist in Medellín and who was I to doubt her? If anyone would know, she would. But I worried about it for the next few days. We decided to track down the owners of Fanny and get her back – that was the only way I could be sure. Any dog with rabies would be dead within ten days of first showing the symptoms and, in any case, I had got an idea of what Fanny's likely problem was from listening to the history and my brief look at her from across the desk. I reckoned she probably had chronic pancreatic insufficiency.

With the help of a bit of sleuthing on Cristina's part, Fanny duly returned and, with a huge muzzle strapped around her mouth, she was trussed up in the usual way – after my last experience I could see the point of it.

She was a good 30 per cent below her proper weight. I had a good prod and feel. In England at the time we were diagnosing pancreatic disease by an examination of the faeces for the enzyme trypsin: today's sophisticated blood tests were a long way off. But at least we had the microscope, which was a rather flash affair and on loan from one of Eduardo's friends.

I did a smear from a sample of Fanny's poo and looked to see what I could make of it. There were a few parasite eggs and a lot of fat globules, which fitted with a diagnosis of pancreatic disease. Cristina tracked down a pharmacist who could dispense pancreatic enzyme pills so Fanny was sent off on treatment with that and a wormer, and the clinic was a hundred pesos better off. I celebrated that night with a slap-up meal in a cheap restaurant in town. Bean stew was becoming a favourite, washed down with a couple of beers.

¡Viva El Vet!

I reflected on my first few days in sole charge. On the downside my leg was sore and I was worrying more than I had ever done before – the joys of running my own business for the first time. However, at the end of only the first week as my own boss I was about to acquire a client who would make a big difference to my finances and largely rid me of the worry as to where my next meal was coming from. Her name was Janina de Schwarzkopf.

In spite of the name she was American but married to a German. Janina was from the Deep South of the USA and dedicated to her dog Bosun, one of the largest boxers I had ever seen. Dedicated is maybe the wrong word – besotted was more like it. Her husband Ernst was regularly away from home, although I didn't find out about that till later. He was another who had arrived shortly after the war and was reticent about his role in it. Neither Janina nor Bosun seemed to take much notice of Ernst. I was sure that she cared a lot more about her dog than about her husband. However, I saw all three for the first time at the end of my first week.

Not for the last time with Bosun, I was to be puzzled as to why his owner had called me in. He was in rude health – he was probably the finest specimen of dog I had seen in my brief time in Colombia. Nonetheless I had instructions to check his teeth, eyes, ears, heart and everything else Janina could think of. The consultation lasted the best part of an hour – not that that mattered too much: this wasn't the Harmsworth where, with a waiting room full of people, a consultation longer than seven minutes scuppered everything for the rest of the day. As nobody else turned up, I could afford to take my time.

Bosun was the most amazingly patient dog. 'He's very good, isn't he?' I said.

Janina positively beamed.

'You know how to say de right dings,' her husband said, in his thick German accent.

'No. Honestly, I mean it.' And I did.

Bosun gave me a lick – I was definitely in.

'Are you available for home visits, Dr Grant?' Janina suddenly said. Home visits? What for? The dog was perfectly all right, as I had already made clear.

'Either Ernst' – here she motioned to her husband – 'or my driver can always pick you up.'

I made a quick calculation – Cristina would have to tell me how much to charge: I didn't think Eduardo did home visits. But with the sound of a cash register ringing in my imagination, there was only one answer. 'Of course,' I said.

'Good. Shall we say next Tuesday, then? And come for lunch. Ernst will pick you up at twelve-thirty, won't you, Liebchen?'

Ernst gave a shrug and a nod.

Things were looking up. Cristina collected the two hundred pesos – a princely sum for declaring that a healthy dog was healthy – and ushered our new clients out with a suitable show of deference.

'Eh, *ave Maria*,' she said, 'Eduardo will be pleased.' Then she went on to tell me that he had phoned from Apartado and she was to pass on the message that he wouldn't be back for a month.

I heard this news with more equanimity than I would have five days earlier. I could give myself Saturday off. I had been invited to Gloria's family *finca* in the foothills of the mountains outside town. There would be a barbecue in beautiful surroundings with the whole family there. I was beginning to find that Colombian hospitality knew no limits. My new life wasn't at all bad.

Chapter 6

Gloria's brother, Jorge, picked me up at ten on Saturday morning and we headed for the hills. The rest of the family were already at the *finca* preparing lunch. It was to be a real gathering of the clans. Three out of the five sisters were there with their husbands: Irma and Gustavo, Lottie and Dario, Yvonne and Diego, and lastly Jorge, who was not yet married. He was the baby of the family and too busy enjoying the good life to think about abandoning his single status just yet.

Each of the sisters had a little of Gloria in their features – I could certainly see the family resemblance – but not her vivacity, perhaps because they had stayed in Colombia while she had gone to England. It seemed miraculous that I was there, and all thanks to her. I felt enormously warm towards her, but no more than that now, I realised.

Each family had brought their maid, and Cousin Clara made up the entourage. Presiding over the whole family were Don Enrique and Doña Matilde.

The *finca* was a large Spanish colonial-style farmhouse with a veranda, which looked over Medellín nestling in the valley far below. The view was astounding. It had rained early in the morning, clearing the air, and the city glistened in the heat of the morning sunshine. There wasn't a cloud in the sky and the buildings were crystal clear. I could just pick out the clinic and, seemingly next door, the start of the main

79

airport runway. A steady stream of planes swooped over the roofs and landed.

The family were an attractive bunch and Don Enrique dispensed drinks while his wife chatted away. I was able to understand about half of what was said.

Gustavo was busy setting up a barbecue. He was probably the best-looking of the lot, and Diego, Yvonne's husband, teased him constantly about the many women he had been out with before settling down with Irma. Gustavo was now managing a farm owned by Don Enrique and they lived comfortably on the edge of town.

Standing on the veranda, with a beer in my hand and looking over the valley, I felt like a millionaire on holiday.

Later, in the garden, the barbecue was soon filling the air with wonderful smells. We had kebabs, which were called *chuzos* and *empanadas*, like samosas. Again I was surprised that nobody seemed to drink wine: it was beer or *aguardiente*.

The conversation ebbed and flowed and after a while I dropped out of it, suffering from the fatigue of struggling in a new language. The debate was animated, though, with each participant taking centre stage to make their point with much gesticulating. So different from the reserved English.

In the background the maids beavered away, removing plates, replenishing drinks and generally being dogsbodies, but with a quiet reserve. It would be some time before I heard their point of view. I felt ashamed when ordering anything from them: I knew how little they were paid – or at least how little Eduardo's maid Maria was paid. Perhaps the Ruiz family was more generous.

My ears and brain tuned in again when the conversation turned to kidnapping. According to Gustavo, who was finishing off the cooking, it wasn't only Don Enrique who was a prime target – any of the family was. 'Probably even you, David, come to that.'

I nearly choked on my beer.

Gustavo laughed. 'They would just suppose you were a rich gringo. They have no imagination, these people. To them all gringos are the same.'

Well, he was certainly right about that.

Although a number of guerrilla groups were operating in Colombia at the time, the most active was the FARC, who were renowned for biding their time. A year in captivity for the victim was nothing while complicated negotiations were conducted. FARC would start with a ransom of a million dollars and end up with whatever could be prised out of the victim's relatives. I shuddered at the thought. If you failed to call attention to yourself from that group there was always the ELN. I couldn't begin to understand their politics, except that it revolved around armed struggle, kidnapping, violence and general dissatisfaction with the status quo.

It transpired that Gustavo had a gun in the car, but that was the only defence we would have if we were attacked. I wondered if I was being teased. Coming from ultra-safe England I didn't pay much heed to what was being said and I was young enough to believe that I was immortal.

'Do not walk in town at night!' said Don Enrique, his finger wagging at me, as the subject changed from national issues to local crime.

'*Muy peligroso*. Very dangerous!' He repeated it in English, as if to emphasise the point. Although none of the Ruiz family was fluent in English, they all spoke a little – as did many educated Colombians. As my Spanish was much better, they never used English with me.

As dusk descended we headed back to the family apartment in the centre of town, high up on the eighth floor. There was a strong sense of relief as we passed the watchman – back to total security, even more food and the finest Scotch whisky, which was Don Enrique's particular weakness. In his late seventies, he was doing well on it. The view at night from here was different from the view from the *finca*, but just as wonderful. I looked out on it from the balcony, standing well back from the edge. Gustavo joined me and gestured to the twinkling lights half-way up the mountain on all sides. '*Tugurios*.' Shanty town. 'Very poor people.'

I had seen glimpses of this world as we came down from the *finca* and said I would like to see more.

'You would not survive five minutes,' he said, but these words of wisdom were all hearsay: it transpired that no one from the family had ever been there. I resolved to get up there and see things for myself. Apparently many of the street children, the *gamines*, came from the *tugurios* having been kicked out by their families for lack of food. They had to fend for themselves from the age of four or five. It seemed hardly possible. Cristina had talked about it, though, so I just nodded. This was another thing I was determined to find out about. Apparently some rich people fed these children like English people fed stray cats at home.

For the moment I was living in the lap of luxury and the only difficulty I had was with whether my work had any relevance in Colombian society. It seemed wrong to be treating pampered pets when all around me I could see extreme poverty and illness due to lack of food and basic medicines.

The point was hammered home to me next morning by my first client. Word seemed to be getting around that the *inglés* would perform miracles. Looking at the Doberman puppy in front of me, miracle was the right word if anything was to be done. Just five months old and his ear-cropping operation had gone wrong. One ear was standing upright in the approved fashion, but the other had become infected and collapsed, giving the dog a lop-eared effect. Eduardo had not performed the original operation: we were the second opinion.

'It has remained very *feo*,' said the owner, a thirty-something beauty from El Poblado suburb. This time I understood she meant ugly. As far as the ear was concerned there was fibrosis and some residual infection. The cartilage had been irreparably damaged and there was nothing I could do apart from prescribe antibiotics.

The puppy's owner began to cry and looked up at me imploringly. She had hoped to show the dog and win prizes. She offered astronomical sums for me to operate. I repeated that there was nothing more to be done. She sniffed and her attitude towards me changed: she became haughty and unapproachable and left, no doubt on her way to a third opinion. I wondered if the next person would be so unscrupulous as to operate. I hoped not. I thought the pup looked quite cute with his lop ear. So what if he couldn't be shown? There was a knock at the clinic door.

'*No hay nada*,' said Cristina, knowing intuitively that it was yet another beggar.

I was beginning to find out how different attitudes were: massive human poverty on one hand while the mega-rich worried because an ear looked wrong. Money was tight for the small middle class, but they brought their animals in, although they did not necessarily do as I asked and often left things until the last moment. Time here was treated differently from what I was used to in England. The Ruiz family had told me never to arrive punctually for a party: it would always start two hours later, even a dinner party. Clients missed appointments by days rather than minutes or hours.

David Grant

A cat was brought in after being run over a week before. I reckoned that it had a pelvic fracture. Eduardo occasionally used the radiographer at the local children's hospital (for a price) but there was no question of having this cat X-rayed. I would have to give an opinion and treat it or put it down for a hundred pesos (negotiable). After an exhausting haggle the cat was taken home for rest and a prayer because I couldn't be sure what I was treating without X-rays.

Later that morning I was due to be picked up by Ernst Schwarzkopf for my first home visit. Just as the owner of the cat was leaving, a toot indicated that Ernst had arrived precisely on time. I was surprised enough to look at my watch. But then I remembered: even though he had lived for twenty years in Colombia, Ernst was German.

He almost clicked his heels as he came in, addressing me as 'Doctor'. I told him to call me David, but Doctor I remained. Although probably in his early sixties, he looked a lot younger. Immaculately dressed, he was obviously concerned about style as we got into his open top Triumph sports car. He professed to being an Anglophile and had business contacts in England, he said. The TR3 was blue and we shot out of the road and through the suburbs to the Retiro district where he lived with Janina who, it turned out, was his second wife. It was her second marriage, too, and I sensed that all was not well between them. Or perhaps it was just Ernst's formality that clashed with Janina's southern mannerisms.

We sped through the suburbs, not bothering to stop at red traffic lights. Everyone jumped them routinely, even Eduardo in his clapped-out Renault. You were rarely caught, Eduardo had explained, and if you were you could always offer the occasional efficient policeman a small bribe, which would resolve the matter. Better that than risk a robbery while waiting for the lights to change.

¡Viva El Vet!

It was as if Ernst was reading my mind. 'Vatch those vagabonds at de next lights.'

A group of about ten *gamines*, all about twelve or thirteen, were hanging around at the next intersection ostensibly to wash windscreens. In the nineties this trade arrived in England, but to me, in 1974, it was a new phenomenon. Ernst sailed through to shouts and curses. He grinned at me. 'Dey say my mudder was a whore.' He laughed. 'How can dey know such dings?'

'Aren't you a bit vulnerable in an open car?' I asked.

'Of course, but in dis country you haf to take – how do you say it? – de rough vid de smooth.'

He put his foot down, pleased with his dominance of the English language. 'I do not allow my vife to drive dis car, it is too dangerous. But I like to take a liddle spin now and den.'

We turned into a side-road from which private roads fanned out. A man with a submachine-gun stopped us at the entrance to one. On seeing Ernst at the wheel he waved us through, having given me a careful look.

'Now ve are in civilization,' said Ernst. 'De vatchman von't allow any undesirables to come vidin a kilometre of the house.' I wondered whether if I hadn't been sitting in the passenger seat of Ernst's TR3 I would have passed muster.

We went down a driveway lined with trees and flowers and eventually, after nearly half a mile, arrived at what looked like the farmhouse in the American TV soap *Dallas*. I half expected JR to jump out at any minute. Ernst pulled a small radio from the dashboard and pressed a button. A large garage door at the side of the house opened. I had never seen anything like it in England. Commonplace now, in 1974 it was revolutionary. Within thirty seconds we had driven through the door, which closed behind us. We were, indeed, in another world. A maid appeared and opened double doors that led into the house.

'Bring us two visky,' Ernst barked in Spanish.

'With ice, please,' I added.

There was no sign of the mistress of the house.

'She's probably out valking de dog,' Ernst judged. 'Ve have enough land for him to have no need of ever leaving de property,' he added, as we went through the lounge to the patio.

If I thought the view from Don Enrique's *finca* was amazing what I saw now put it completely in the shade. Immaculately nurtured lawns led down to a massive collection of flowers bordered by trees with the backdrop of the Andes all around. It was a beautifully still day without a cloud in the sky, the temperature climbing to 25°C, a little hotter than usual. The whiskies arrived on a silver tray with some canapés.

'You like caviar?' Ernst said. I had never even seen it before.

A distant barking announced the imminent arrival of Bosun. Janina was pleased to see me and so was Bosun – he came straight to me, wagging what was his tail stump, ignoring his master.

'Dat dog has no brains,' said Ernst.

Janina gave him a warning look: nobody criticised her dog. She picked up a caviar-laden biscuit and tossed it at Bosun. He caught it mid-air and swallowed it in a millisecond.

Ernst looked at this exercise disdainfully, then turned to me. 'Dis is not good for dogs, *nichts*?'

The wisdom of giving dogs caviar had never before featured in my veterinary question-and-answer sessions.

'But you only have to look at Bosun to see it's good

for him,' Janina protested. 'Look at his coat. Caviar is like his vitamins. He has some every day and you said only last week that he was in perfect condition,' she added, turning to me for confirmation. 'And you are, aren't you, Bosie?'

When Ernst went into the house to take a phone call his wife elaborated on her routine with Bosun. 'He likes to sleep at the bottom of the bed – but only when Ernst isn't around.' I gathered that this was frequently.

'And he likes tea and toast for breakfast.' She pronounced toast with an exaggerated 'O' which sounded more like 'eh-o' that some Americans do. 'And afterwards I always clean his mouth and his . . .' here she searched for the appropriate word '. . . his butt.' She spoke shyly in a little-girl voice, as though I might disapprove. I nodded. I had seen too much first at Canterbury and then at the Harmsworth to be surprised by anything – though it must be said that Colombian dog etiquette was as bizarre as anything I had encountered.

'He's doing well,' I said, thinking I would have to start earning my fee, but before any examination could begin lunch was served.

We ate *al fresco* among the stunning scenery with fine wines from Germany. A delicious bean soup was followed by a chicken dish with all sorts of vegetables I hadn't seen before and, finally, a tropical fruit salad. We finished with fine French Cognac and coffee. I hadn't eaten so well since leaving Canterbury.

It was a rather mellow veterinary surgeon who cast an eye over Bosun. There was, of course, nothing wrong with him, but I arranged to visit again to administer a worming treatment and get his vaccinations up to date. About five in the evening I staggered out with ten dollars in my pocket and some pesos to pay for a taxi home.

Ernst was busy on the phone and in any case the Triumph was back in its garage, not to be brought out for a few months.

I arrived back at the clinic to see a large Cadillac outside. Almost at once Cristina shot out to let me in, shaking her wrist and looking all agitated. 'Eh, *ave Maria*, Hector is here. He is Mafia.'

She crossed herself and hid in the operating room as Pilar came out with a flash-looking man of about thirty-five. He was expensively dressed and tanned with the heaviest gold watch on his wrist I had ever seen. When he laughed you could see several gold fillings. They invited me into the house to have an *aguardiente* and dismissed Cristina, who shot out and went home without a backward glance.

Hector had brought his guitar with him and no sooner had we sat down in what I still thought of as Eduardo's lounge, than he picked it up and launched into a couple of the old favourites that you could hear outside any open-air bar or restaurant. First, '*La Ruana*', a song about the traditional poncho, and then a lively upbeat version of '*Pueblito Viejo*', which brought Eduardo to mind even more strongly.

I had still not got to the bottom of Cristina's idea that Hector was *mafioso*. As far as I could see he was just a talented musician and, judging from the way he looked, probably a professional. I was wrong. However, he clearly used his talent to woo women and, judging by Pilar's reaction, his efforts were successful. After a couple of *aguardientes* – Eduardo's, no doubt – he suggested we all go into town and have some fun. By this time my normal reticence in these matters had flown – I had already had whisky, Gewürztraminer, Cognac and *aguardiente*, so why not make a day of it?

We all piled into the Cadillac, Hector gave the driver,

Pablo, instructions and we headed into the centre. Leaving Pablo, who was more like a bodyguard, to park the car we walked up the Pasaje Junin, which was bustling with young people. Whether the regular shouts of '*Bizcocho*' in our direction were for Hector or me, there was no telling. We wandered up towards the *Aleros del Parque*, a small restaurant overlooking the Pasaje where we could eat and watch the action. There, we had a typical Antioquian meal with *arepas*, the maize cakes, chicken with *frijoles* and beer. Hector had his eyes on the beautiful women and Pilar didn't seem to notice or care, contenting herself with pouring his beer each time another arrived. We finished our meal and walked back to where the driver was waiting. We sped out of the centre to the smart suburb of El Poblado, to Carrera 43 – Street 43. Medellín's streets were built on a grid, which made it quite easy to find your way about. It appeared that Hector had decided to take us to his nightclub. It was the first I knew about this side of his business life. 'So,' I said, 'is this what you do?'

He looked at me sardonically.

'As a living,' I went on, 'to make money.'

He didn't seem to understand what I was getting at. Then he laughed as if I had made an joke. 'No, no, *amigo*. Import-export,' he said, flashing a golden grin.

My first impression of the nightclub was that it was very discreet and very dark. The doorman jumped out of his skin when he saw who had arrived and took us to a table himself, using a torch to guide us. A bottle of *aguardiente* arrived and some *empanadas*. I couldn't resist these and helped myself: even though I had eaten two large meals that day, tomorrow might be different.

The only light was from a small dance area in which I made out half a dozen entwined couples moving to the rhythm of a salsa band. In the meantime Hector and Pilar were all over each other. I felt like a gooseberry.

As if reading my mind Hector remarked that it was a pity Pilar's sister wasn't with us. I had met her once, and although she was only eighteen she had seemed older. She was a great improvement on Pilar and it was hard to imagine they were related.

Hector and Pilar spent some time smooching, leaving me to my own devices. I listened to the music, which was good. The Colombians were particularly good at salsa. I had already heard excellent accordion-based music, called *vallenatos*, plus this salsa type, which really made you want to dance even if you had no idea how to do it. Suddenly a tango struck up and the lights in the centre came on so that I could see all around. There were lots of tables, with one or two couples sitting at them with plates of food and the obligatory bottle of *aguardiente* – did Colombians drink anything else? Suddenly only one couple was on the dance floor, Hector and Pilar, dancing the swirling, entwined tango. While their bodies were tightly clasped together, their legs were flashing in and out, here and there. I was impressed.

I remembered vaguely that Gloria had once told me that the tango outside its native Argentina was most popular here in Medellín. Suddenly all eyes were on the two dancers. They were obviously practised at it, as they were step perfect. The band played on, and the dance seemed to go on for ever. When it stopped the couple kissed and thunderous applause erupted. As they took their bows two swarthy men in dark sunglasses approached Hector and said something in his ear. He frowned and escorted Pilar back to our table. 'I must go,' he said, with a slight bow. 'A business matter,' he added. 'Stay for however long you want – Pablo will take you back.' And he was gone, escorted by the two tough-looking men. As they walked out people parted before them looking scared. The aura of menace was almost palpable, and I wondered what the 'business' might be. I asked Pilar. She shrugged her shoulders, took another swig of *aguardiente* and suggested we might dance.

That was the last thing on my mind. I was pleased when, a few minutes later, she yawned and summoned Pablo.

The limousine sped out of El Poblado down the Avenida San Diego, and within minutes we were in our suburb. On the way we passed a traffic accident and I was sure I heard gunshots above the wailing police sirens. At the sound Pablo put his foot down and Pilar clung to me as the dial on the speedo rose to well about 120 k.p.h.

We arrived in one piece and as soon as we were safely inside, Pablo having watched the door open and shut, Maria was summoned from her slumber to fetch two *tintos*. In the background I could hear her young son, not yet christened and apparently without a name, crying. He was only a year old. Maria was lucky to have even this job as a single mother was pretty low on the social scale.

Chapter 7

A day or so later I was sitting idly in the clinic reading *El Mundo*, another Colombian daily. It suddenly occurred to me how like Eduardo I was becoming. I came across a section of the newspaper called *'sucesos breves'* – a kind of news in brief. It was a veritable catalogue of murders, accidents and other kinds of sudden death. A bus had turned over, two cars had collided – I was reminded of the mayhem that was driving in general, and buses in particular. Then followed a litany of shootings and stabbings. One in particular caught my eye that morning.

Two 'delinquents' had been shot dead in El Poblado just after midnight – exactly the same time as we had been there. The police attributed it to a falling-out of drug-dealers, as the two dead youths were well known for their involvement in the trade. Although some names were mentioned, Hector's wasn't, but everything about his sudden departure and its timing suggested his involvement. The expression on his face and those of his henchmen as they left the nightclub had spoken volumes.

Cristina's instincts must be right. I decided to make myself scarce whenever he showed up. I also decided to make sure that Pilar and I were never alone together. Thank goodness I hadn't taken her up on the offer of a tango. Since Eduardo's departure, I had missed the early-morning alarm call of his daily target practice, though even he had seemed intimidated by the power and influence of his wife's boyfriend. No wonder he had removed himself to the remote jungle.

Later that morning I asked Cristina why she was so sure Hector was Mafia.

'The car,' she replied, 'and the watch.' It seemed that even the very rich shunned an ostentatious American limousine: it was a kind of badge, membership of the club of the extreme rich. The watch showed that you were safe from petty theft – in Hector's case, Pablo almost certainly carried a gun and the two hard men in the nightclub had bulges in their jackets.

Reading the papers and talking to ordinary Colombians, it seemed that the Mafia were all-powerful. Police and politicians were in their pockets due to the fabulous sums of money available as bribes and sweeteners. These people were effectively above the law and only feared their own kind. Killings were an everyday occurrence and the reports in the local papers emphasised to ordinary folk the need to keep their own counsel.

That afternoon I was reminded again, as if I needed reminding, that life could be cheap and dangerous. Yet another German shepherd dog arrived in yet another four-wheel-drive jeep. The manager of a wealthy farmer in Envigado, not far from Hector's nightclub on the outskirts of Medellín, had been instructed by his boss to bring in one of the guard dogs. It was panting and stressed.

'What's happened?' I asked

The *mayordomo* shrugged. 'He attacked some *ladrones*. They were trying to steal from the house. One shot the dog. But we have had our revenge.' His eyes lit up. I flashed a look at Cristina.

He misread the shock on my face as concern. 'Don't worry,' he said. 'They are both dead. See what you can do with him.' He gestured towards the panting dog. 'Or he can have the same fate as the *ladrónes*. It's up to you.'

I was about to tell him that I had no experience of gunshot wounds but something told me this was not a good idea. The dog's name was Fidel, he told us. He had obviously lived up to his name, not that that appeared to have impressed the *mayordomo*, who gave us a sardonic smile and left saying that he would be back in two hours. Cristina shuddered and drew up some anaesthetic solution.

A small puncture wound in the dog's side was oozing blood, but there was no exit wound. If he had been shot the bullet was evidently still there. I would have to do something drastic. I lifted his upper lip to have a look at the lining of his mouth, which should have been salmon pink but was getting paler by the minute. By chance Cristina had been down to the children's hospital a few days before and purloined some fluid to give into the vein, in a situation such as this.

Armed with the bag of rehydrating solution and a prayer I cut into the dog's abdomen. Almost immediately there was a welling of blood but the source was soon apparent: the spleen had been almost cut in two and I would have to remove it – which I had done many times at the Harmsworth. A ruptured spleen was not uncommon, sometimes the result of a road-traffic accident, but more often caused by cancer of the spleen. With sophisticated anaesthetic machines and all the paraphernalia of a hospital set-up behind me, it rarely presented problems.

Here, all I had was the ever-patient Cristina topping up the thiopentone solution every time the dog showed signs of coming round. The spleen came out quite quickly and there, floating around in the abdomen, was a bullet, which I removed. I checked all the other organs but found no other damage. Half an hour later I finished sewing up and Fidel was coming round.

'Eh, *ave Maria*,' said Cristina. 'This I have never seen – and it will live!' she added, patting the dog's head.

Maria brought us a *tinto* each – to my shame I had begun to ask her to do things for me – and we settled down to see if Fidel would make a smooth recovery.

'We never operate on shot dogs normally,' Cristina remarked.

Now she tells me, I thought.

'Eduardo was always worried that he would end up the same way – particularly if things went wrong.'

But Fidel was made of stern stuff, or so it seemed: after an hour he was sitting up, resting, and no longer in much pain. Cristina telephoned the *mayordomo* to give him the good news, then typed up some painkillers and antibiotics for him on the pad that Eduardo had signed before he left. I was still not officially allowed to practise on my own account as there was no sign of my work visa.

An hour or so later the *mayordomo* arrived, accompanied by a small plump man in a light suit with very dark sunglasses. From the deferential way in which the *mayordomo* spoke to him, I gathered that this was the boss.

'You the English guy?' he said to me, in faultless American-English.

I said I was, and took him into the consulting room, where Fidel was coming round nicely now, and gave him the bullet. As he inspected it a scowl came across his face and he turned to the *mayordomo* and said in Spanish, 'If only one of those sons-of-bitches were still alive I would have watched them eat this bullet.'

I could feel the blood drain from my face.

He introduced himself as Jaime Ochoa and pulled out a

wad of notes that made Cristina eyes pop and paid twice the normal sum for a laparotomy. 'I will pay the same again if you will come back with us now and supervise the full recovery.'

He led me by the elbow and walked towards the jeep. I looked at Cristina, who just nodded – with 'For God's sake don't argue' written in her eyes.

After carefully lifting Fidel into the back of the jeep, we shot off at top speed towards Envigado, on the outskirts of Medellín, where my new clients lived. I felt like remonstrating with the driver for the sake of the dog but, after a second or two's consideration, thought better of it.

We soon arrived in a salubrious part of town with huge ranch houses hidden behind parkland trees. On the way the police had flagged us down. Roadblocks were quite common and the rule was to be polite and submit patiently to a search for drugs. But not if you were Jaime.

First came a grin, then a profanity. 'Haven't you got eyes? We are taking my dog home after emergency surgery. This English gentleman is the doctor.'

The young, wary-looking cops were fingering the triggers on their automatic rifles. This did not seem to worry Jaime, who produced a bundle of notes from where the others had originated. The more senior cop looked nervously over his shoulder and told him to roll up the notes into a smaller bundle so that the transfer would be less obvious. In a second he had pocketed the money then after a peremptory, slightly exaggerated walk about the car, he waved us on with a salute.

Jaime gave a contemptuous chuckle as we accelerated away. 'Sons-of-bitches,' he said using the more profane Spanish.

A few minutes later we were driving down to his ranch. A

couple of men in tracksuits with machine-guns and snarling German shepherds at their heels waved us through. There was a large paddock at the side of the house, where half a dozen young thoroughbred horses were being schooled. Further to the left two uniformed staff were tending a fifty-metre pool in immaculate condition.

Fidel was lifted out and taken into the house. Large oil paintings adorned most of the walls and maids in uniform scuttled here and there with the arrival of Jaime. Two large whiskies on the rocks appeared and we sat down by the pool. It was pure Hollywood. We were soon joined by Jaime's wife, a stunning young woman of about my age – her husband, I guessed, was about ten years older.

Yolanda did not speak English, and did not seem concerned about the dog. I had become used to the women being far more attached to their pets than the men, but Fidel, I now knew, was not a pet: he was just one of the guard dogs. Although she was very beautiful, it was soon apparent that Yolanda was not as well educated as her husband. After a while she grew bored with trying to get me to understand her thick *paisa* accent and disappeared, then reappeared in a bikini and dived into the water. I took care not to glance at her. I knew enough about *paisa* men not to insult them by ogling their women, no matter how incredible they looked. And Yolanda could have won a Miss World contest, except for the bit where they had to talk about their ambitions. Her ambition was already fulfilled, I suspected – no dreams there of saving the whale or becoming an eye surgeon.

When I asked how come he spoke such good English, Jaine told me he had been to school in New York and still had many friends and 'business contacts' there. Foolishly I ventured to ask the nature of his business. It would have been rude not to. 'Chemicals,' was his reply – and his face hardened. I did not push it any further.

While we were talking, the maid had been laying a table in the shade of some trees. When the food arrived I lost no time in tucking in. 'Hmm,' I said appreciatively. '*Sancocho de gallina.*' This was a steaming bowl of thick soup with bits of chicken, rice, corn, plantain and yucca that I had had before. 'Antioquian style,' I added, for good measure.

This was safer territory than 'chemicals'.

'You like the food from Antioquia?' he asked. I could see he was amused that an Englishman knew anything about Colombian food. But I had eaten in many cheap local restaurants now and I was becoming an expert. The *comida corriente* – everyday menu – available everywhere consisted of meat, *arepas*, salad, fried plantain and *frijoles*. After bean stew this thick country soup was my favourite. As we ate, the sun set rapidly over the mountains.

'*Paraíso – no es cierto?*' It is paradise, don't you think? he said, reverting to Spanish.

I nodded in agreement, but at the same time wondered how often there were shootouts in these grounds. In the distance I could see a couple of watchmen patrolling the main entrance from the road.

When we finished, I suggested I take a look at Fidel. We walked into the huge ranch-style kitchen where a cook and assorted staff were busying around. No sign of *la señora* but Fidel was sitting up having eaten a bowl of scraps the cook had given him. His colour was amazingly better than it had been a few hours earlier.

'He's a tough dog,' I said, stroking his head. 'He'll make it. But now I have to go,' I added, in what I hoped was a businesslike manner. 'I need to check up on a couple of patients.' A lie. I was thinking more of Cristina, whom I had left in a state of near terror and who, if I didn't return soon, would imagine I had been abducted, or worse.

Jaime called over the *mayordomo* and told him to drive me back. 'Take the gun,' he said, handing him a large pistol. 'Better to take precautions.' He grinned at me, having seen the fear on my face. 'Don't look so shocked, Doc. Everyone has them here,' he said. 'And, hey, *amigo*,' he punched my shoulder, 'you saved us a lot of money this morning. Thanks for your good work. We'll have you take a look at the horses next time.'

Before I could admit to my ignorance of horses the *mayordomo* and I were on our way at great speed out of Envigado, heading for El Poblado where the majority of my rich clients lived. I sat in the front of the jeep with the loaded revolver lying beside me and was relieved when we pulled up outside the house.

Cristina was still in the clinic. She was flicking her wrist in anguish at the thought of what might have happened.

'But Jaime seems very civilised,' I said. 'His English is perfect – he even sounds like an American.'

'You don't understand, Dr David, these are dangerous people.' Cristina's eyes were wide with fear.

I thought she was exaggerating. I was wrong.

Anyway, Christmas was coming. I had been in Medellín for nearly three months. My visa would run out on 10 January. Cristina had good news on that score: a letter had arrived at midday from the immigration authorities, she said. I had been told to pick up my visa from Cúcuta any time after 1 January. Soon I would be legally in the country.

A letter from Eduardo told me that he had decided to come back for a few weeks at Christmas in an attempt to patch up his marriage. Fat chance, I thought, having seen

Hector working his magic. Frankly, I still couldn't see the appeal of Pilar – Hector could have had his pick. For all I knew, perhaps he still did. The bonus of Eduardo coming back would be that I could take a holiday before starting work on my own again. Gloria's family, it turned out, had plans for me at Christmas.

It seemed to me that the whole of Medellín – at least the affluent part – took off an entire month at Christmas. This meant that the clinic was even quieter than usual. Some days we were lucky to have any clients at all. After a while I was in real Eduardo mode, spending the whole morning reading *El Colombiano*, which was good for my Spanish but bad for keeping up to date with animal disease. It had been quite a relief when, in his letter, Eduardo suggested that I should take three weeks off – unpaid, of course.

From wondering how I was going to get to the *finca* they had been talking about for the couple of days I'd been expecting to have off, everything was now simple. I could travel there and back with the family.

It was in the department of Córdoba, about 180 kilometres to the north of Medellín. The *finca*, which belonged to some friends, was on the side of a tropical lake called Ayapel, near to a town called Caucasia, about half-way between Medellín and Cartagena up on the Caribbean coast. I was soon taken up in the excitement of all the arrangements.

We would stay there for a week. Although you could fly to Caucasia with a local airline, we were going to drive, a real adventure, which would take nine hours through the jungle. I was assured I would have to pay for nothing. It was amazing hospitality, and I knew I could never repay it.

On the first day of the holiday, though, Doña Matilde wanted to take me to an orphanage on the outskirts of Medellín that the family had founded called El Hogar

Infantil. The two of us arrived unannounced and I was staggered to see 160 children there, ranging from three to ten years old. It was the youngest who upset me. They were all suffering from varying degrees of starvation, the worst pot-bellied with emaciation. It was the disease called kwashiorkor, due to simple lack of protein, which I'd heard of in Africa but hadn't believed to exist in Colombia.

The babies, Doña Matilde told me, as we walked around the orphanage, were often not orphans in the sense that their parents had died but had been abandoned, particularly if they were girls, because their families couldn't feed them. Don Enrique paid for food and medical attention, and tried to save their lives, although some died soon after arriving. They would then try to have them adopted. Sometimes the children's parents would reclaim them once they had improved, but it wasn't unheard-of for children to arrive in a poor state several times in a year.

I was shocked by what I saw and by the news that for every child in the orphanage there were almost certainly ten in the *tugurios* – the shanty towns. But at least Don Enrique was trying to do something – if only there were more like him.

A total contrast followed.

We set off two days before Christmas. All of Gloria's sisters, except the one who was in the States, came with their husbands and, of course, Don Enrique and his wife, and three maids.

The road was reasonable to start with but deteriorated rapidly as we descended into the hot lands, as they called them. But the countryside was beautiful, a land of lakes and waterfalls. Within only a couple of hours we had reached sea level, a drop of five thousand feet, and I was reminded of how near we were to the equator. The heat was stifling and there was nothing to do but grin and bear it. After what seemed an interminable journey we arrived at nightfall and unpacked.

The *finca* was enormous. I had my own room and, amazingly, it was air-conditioned – absolute bliss. Parrots glided from tree to tree and monkeys whooped in warning. As soon as everyone had settled in, we all piled into the swimming-pool and then were fed a sumptuous meal prepared by the maids, followed by beer, *aguardiente* and more food.

The guilt I had felt on leaving the orphanage was over-come by an alcoholic haze. The conversation livened up over the drink. Gustavo, who had seen more poverty than the rest of the family as he wasn't from a wealthy background, thought the problem of the *tugurios* was insoluble, short of some left-wing revolution. The others shivered at the thought of left-wingers and what they would do if they ever came to power.

'Did you know that M19 guerrillas are active in this area?' Gustavo went on. Kidnapping was his favourite topic of conversation. I had never once been in his company without the subject cropping up.

An argument then developed as to whether this was true. The M19 was one of three revolutionary groups that controlled remote parts of the country and specialised in kidnappings.

Gustavo was adamant. 'The owners of this *finca* were kidnapped three years ago,' he volunteered. 'You haven't forgotten, surely?' Gustavo followed politics more closely than the rest of the family.

Unnervingly, this turned out to be true. The owners *had* been kidnapped and eventually freed after a year – on payment of a large ransom. It hadn't gone to plan because the police and the army had been tipped off. The son of the owner had lost an eye in a shootout when the switch occurred. The guerrillas got away unscathed with the money.

Gustavo's wife, Irma, cast a concerned look at me in case I was worried about my imminent kidnapping. 'It was three years ago,' she said. 'There has been nothing around here since then. They have moved up to Turbo, I read it in the paper.'

Turbo was a rough frontier port, dealing mainly in bananas on the Gulf of Uraba, on the Caribbean coast.

'Well, if they come here, they will pick the rich gringo.' Gustavo laughed, indicating me.

I burst out laughing myself at this. If only you knew, I thought. 'A year in the jungle with a left-wing guerrilla group would be fascinating – worth a book.' I laughed again but they didn't. Somehow, the very real danger of subversive groups never touched my consciousness and I crashed out that night before my head touched the pillow.

Chapter 8

Ayapel was a beautiful place, untouched by tourism. It was just as Gabriel Garcia Marquez wrote, 'a paradise of dampness and silence, going back to before original sin'.

Trees with brightly coloured blossom proved a draw for birds, including tiny hummingbirds no more than two inches long that I thought at first were butterflies because their wings moved so fast.

Most people seemed poor but happy. Some people in the village lived in mud huts such as you might see in Africa and lived mostly by fishing in the lake. There was no real need to leave the *finca*. Food had been brought from Medellín and we could catch fish for supper. The first morning was spent doing just that and I caught several large fish the like of which I had never seen before, which were cooked at that night's barbecue. The next morning, Christmas Day, I distinguished myself by teaching Yvonne's son Pablo how to swim. He was five, and a little rascal with short hair no more than an inch long that stood up like a brush. He looked a bit like a young Mickey Dolenz in *Circus Boy*, one of the first television programmes I ever watched when I was a boy growing up in Kent.

Pablo knew no fear and trusted the gringo more than his father Diego. But the shoe was on the other foot later that afternoon when Diego offered to teach me to water-ski. Lake Ayapel was plenty big enough for a motorboat to go full pelt for quite a long way, although not so big that you couldn't see the other side. The shore was muddy and the water was a bit murky.

Anyway, Diego had found out that there was a speedboat at the *finca* and at the back of the boathouse he had also discovered a pair of serviceable water-skis. A bit of research elicited a boat-driver in the shape of the *finca*'s resident caretaker-watchman.

'Get your ass out of the water,' Diego shouted, as I floated somewhere in the middle of the lake, trying to keep the tips of the two skis above the surface. Diego had spent some time in Texas and had learned some choice expressions, none of which could be understood by anyone but me. This was a mild example.

And Diego's teaching technique was reduced to just this: telling me to get my ass out of the water as the driver revved up the boat. Although the water was cloudy, it was pleasant – like a warm bath – and you could stay in it for hours. It didn't take me long to get the idea. It's mainly a question of hanging on at the beginning and keeping your arms straight and your knees bent. For two hours Diego and I took it in turns to tear up the lake at great speed. Even high-speed crashes didn't worry me – after all, I was guaranteed a soft, warm landing. I had found a great sport. That evening we ate a huge feast and drank well into the night.

Fortunately my skin wasn't too lily white as I had acquired the basis of a good tan in Spain before arriving in South America. A few days of equator sun had done the trick and I looked almost like a local, which was a good thing: looking like a gringo was not a good idea on many counts.

The next morning I couldn't wait to get back in the boat and Diego was delighted to have found a fellow devotee. We had a morning session and an afternoon session, while the rest of the family hung around the pool.

As we were mooring the boat at the end of the day I asked Gustavo why he hadn't joined us. It was just the sort of thing I had imagined he would enjoy.

'It's the rays,' he said.

'I wouldn't have thought your skin would burn,' I said. Concern about skin cancer was in its infancy in the early seventies.

'Not the sun's rays,' he said, with more of a grimace than a grin. 'Sting rays.' He did a mime with his hands of a fish swimming through the water. I looked back at the suddenly ominous-looking lake.

'Don't take any notice of him,' Diego butted in. 'These things are only a problem if you're in the shallows and you tread on them. Then the tail comes up like this,' and he did a crude gesture with his arm, 'and you get a sting in the *cojones* – rarely fatal, though, according to what I have heard.' I suddenly felt unwell. But, as usual, I couldn't be sure if they were just winding me up. Yet, as they kept reminding me, we were in 'hot country', as the Colombians called the tropics. The story was plausible. What did I know?

Every now and then as we were sitting by the pool an iguana would flit across the garden and shoot up a tree. Small monkeys were always hanging around whenever there was any food and glimpsed dozens of brightly coloured birds that I had only previously seen in zoos. The area was alive with wildlife. At night the noises took over. When I was young one of my favourite books had been *The Wind in the Willows*, and the Wild Wood had always seemed the ultimate in terror. Yet here I was in a wilder wood than Kenneth Grahame could ever have experienced. It should have been frightening, but was curiously reassuring.

We hardly ventured into the village, except to buy beers

from the local bar. The local people were friendly and if they were jealous of our opulence they didn't show it.

In spite of all the wild life and potential dangers like the sting rays, the only mishap involved a colony of ants that Pablo stumbled into. He had been playing beside the swimming pool, hardly having left it since he had learned to swim, when he started to play with an ants' nest. The next thing I knew he was crying and furiously scratching his arms and legs. Great weals had suddenly appeared and his eyelids began to puff up. I had seen similar reactions in dogs and knew that he was suffering from an allergic reaction and needed to see a doctor. Fortunately that didn't present a problem because every doctor in Colombia has to spend his or her first year after qualification in the country, usually in a remote village. Within minutes Pablo had been transported to the village and the doctor's clinic, which was handily situated in the pharmacy.

The doctor was older than I had expected – I had thought we would find a young, keen, newly qualified student type. But this man was an Eduardo lookalike: short, overweight and rather sad-looking. They might have been twins. He confirmed my diagnosis immediately then proceeded to dispense half a dozen different remedies, including a couple of injections. These had to be administered by a paramedic specialising in injections, called a *practicante*, attached to the pharmacy. I reckoned that, in similar circumstances, a dog would have needed a jab of steroid or antihistamine at most but here, just as in Eduardo's clinic, polypharmacy was the rule.

Poor Pablo was carried back to the *finca* crying from the irritation caused by the ant bites, the pain of several injections and the vile taste of whatever had been poured down his throat, two-thirds of which, in my view, had been unnecessary. But by seven in the evening he was well on the way to recovery and everybody was relieved because early the next morning it was time to go home.

When I arrived back in Medellin Eduardo was nowhere in evidence. We had set off early from the *finca* and it was late afternoon. After I had taken my bags up to my room I looked for Maria. I found her in her room and she told me that she had seen neither Eduardo nor Pilar. I wondered whether I should take off any more time, but Eduardo might return at any moment and, anyway, I was on my way to Cali, which vies with Medellín for the title of second city of Colombia.

The previous week I had had a call from Bertica, Henry Garcia's wife. She was back in Colombia for Christmas. Henry had stayed in London but – as she always did – Bertica had brought the two children with her to see their grandparents. Would I like to come for a few days, she said. I certainly would. Cali was in the south of Colombia, towards the border with Ecuador. As I tucked into Maria's simple meal of chicken and rice I thought, not for the first time, of how lucky I had been with my Colombian friends. Since Henry had started working at the Harmsworth, I had got to know Bertica very well and without her I wouldn't have got my Spanish O level, of that I was convinced.

Suddenly there was an urgent knocking at the door and, without thinking, I opened it: it would probably be Eduardo who had misplaced his keys – which he did regularly, particularly after a heavy session with a bottle of *aguardiente*.

But it was an elegant woman of about thirty. 'You are the doctor?'

Although I was officially on holiday there was only one answer to that.

¡Viva El Vet!

'I have a sick dog – she cannot give birth.'

The dog, a German shepherd, was in her car. I was on holiday, but a vet is like a doctor: you are never really on holiday. I went with her to have a look. The dog was in a very bad way indeed. 'How long has she been in labour?' I asked.

'About a week.'

A week? Why hadn't they sought help before now?

She shrugged. 'On holidays.'

I didn't believe it for a moment. It was the usual thing of not wanting to spend money on a vet.

The dog's name was Bonita, she said, as I picked her up and carried her in. She looked half dead. Unlike many of the Colombian dogs I had encountered hitherto she made no objection to being examined. 'She'll need an immediate operation,' I said, which was true – and a Caesarian is something I wouldn't have thought twice about at the Harmsworth. But as soon as the words left my mouth I realised what I had let myself in for.

Cristina was on holiday. It was just me, Maria – who had gone back to her room – and this elegant woman. Forget Maria. I heard her little boy crying. Waves of panic engulfed me. 'You will have to help me,' I said. She nodded dumbly.

I searched around the clinic for what I needed, cursing the fact that I didn't even know where Cristina lived.

If I had to tell her what I do, I needed to know the woman's name. I asked her what it was.

'Emma,' she said. I was startled. It seemed such an unlikely Jane Austen name for a place like Medellín.

I found a pack of instruments, some anaesthetic, rope ties and some clippers. I was ready to go. I showed Emma how to bring the vein up in the front leg and gave Bonita 5 cc of anaesthetic. A dog of this size would normally need 15 cc, but she was so weak from her prolonged labour that she needed only a third of the normal dose.

Within seconds she was deeply asleep. It was all too much for Emma who said she felt faint and went to sit in the other room. I would have to work without her.

I went at it like a demon, clipping the hair, sterilising the skin, and then began to open her up. Once inside the abdomen I found that the womb had ruptured with some dead puppies protruding. As quickly as I could I removed everything. Suddenly I realised I had forgotten to get ready the suture material to sew her up. I gave her another 2 cc of anaesthetic and went hunting for it, praying that I would find some. That's what comes of trusting someone so implicitly as I did Cristina. The idea that I would have to find things on my own had not occurred to me.

My prayers were answered when I found some in a cupboard in the office. Emma was sitting on my chair, her head in her hands, whether from remorse at not bringing Bonita in before or squeamishness, I couldn't tell. I had an overwhelming temptation to shout at her for leaving it so long but thought better of it and scrubbed up again before I sewed up. A jab of penicillin, and I had done everything I could. I looked at the sad, inert form in front of me. No question of Bonita going home – she would have to stay with me.

But I had a flight to Cali already booked for tomorrow. It left at 2 o'clock.

'I will have to look after her tonight,' I said, 'but promise me you will be here at ten, English time, tomorrow morning. I have a plane to catch.'

She nodded. 'Will she live?'

'I honestly don't know.' And I honestly didn't.

¡Viva El Vet!

A few minutes after she'd gone I realised I had taken no details, no name, no address, not to mention a fee. Cristina usually handled that side of things.

Meantime Bonita was showing signs of coming round. I marvelled at the resilience of these country German shepherds, used to living outside all year round. More than a week giving birth – must be some kind of record I thought to myself. I got some blankets and settled down in the office to wait, but I was so shattered that the next time I opened my eyes it was six in the morning. Bonita had staggered over to my side during the night and was sleeping peacefully beside me. As I stirred she woke up and licked my face.

I got up, found a bowl and gave her some water. Just then Maria walked in. 'You English, you are mad,' she said, eyeing the dog apprehensively. To her Bonita looked like one of the many thousands of guard dogs in the city. But she bustled out and soon brought in some scrambled eggs, which I ate greedily. Bonita was sniffing the air so I asked Maria to make some more – I didn't say it was for the dog. It disappeared in two seconds flat.

With no one to look after her, I decided to leave Bonita in the operating room and tied her up to the operating table. Then I went upstairs, had a shower and started packing for my long weekend. I had said ten 'English time', which meant on the dot. Even the Colombians know that their attitude to time is a little eccentric – they see it as a joke. Adding two hours is standard practice. But when they need to be punctual, they emphasise it by saying 'English time'.

At eleven I was anxious. By twelve I was extremely anxious and very cross. Then, at five past, I heard a blast on a car horn and looked out of the window. The jeep looked familiar but it wasn't the car Emma had come in the day before. Although, yes, that was indeed Emma. And with her a figure I remembered only too well. The man who I first bargained with, Pedro Ramirez.

'*Hola*, Doctor!' he said, extending his hand palm outermost. 'How is the patient?'

'She'll live.' Amazingly, I thought.

Emma gasped and clapped her hands – she clearly hadn't been expecting that.

'How much do I owe you?'

'Five thousand pesos,' I said. A figure plucked out of the air and doubled.

He laughed. 'But, Doctor, my wife tells me you have removed the womb, no?' He looked at Emma for confirmation. 'Now she cannot breed again. This will cost money. Two thousand pesos.'

I resisted the temptation to punch him in the face. 'Three thousand five hundred pesos. I stayed up with her all night.'

Pedro considered this. 'But she could still die – three thousand. This is more than fair.'

'Three thousand, and take me to the airport now. I have to go to Cali.'

'Cali? This is where the most beautiful women in Colombia are to be found. There are as many as this.' He put his fingers together, somehow indicating quantity. Emma affected indifference – no doubt used to the machismo.

'Well,' he continued, as I stood my ground, 'if you are going to Cali I can't resist.'

He pulled out an enormous wad of notes, peeled off three thousand pesos, bundled the dog, his wife and me into the jeep, then set off at full speed for the airport.

I couldn't believe it, so much money – I would have been happy with half that. Perhaps there was something in this bargaining caper after all.

¡Viva El Vet!

Before leaving the clinic I had written out a prescription and handed it to Emma. 'Don't forget to bring Bonita back in ten days for the stitches to come out, give her the antibiotics and make sure she rests,' I reminded them, as I jumped out and made my way to the check-in counter. With a cheery wave they were off.

An odd couple, I thought: one beautiful elegant young woman and the other a cowboy hippie. He must have *plata*, I reckoned – silver, slang for money in Colombia. With a jolt I realised I had been thinking in Spanish – progress at last. I strode happily to the SAM check-in for the Cali-bound flight.

As she had promised, Bertica met me at Palmaseca airport with Alejandro, who had grown into quite a little boy since I had last seen him, and Claudia. Bertica had the most perfect manners of anyone I have ever met and combined Colombian beauty with European *savoir-faire*. She was very Latin looking, with not a trace of the look of the indigenous people. The upper class in Colombia were always careful to keep the line pure, as they liked to describe it.

The car was parked close to the arrivals hall. Bertica's parents lived about twenty kilometres south of the town so first we drove through Cali itself. Cali has a very different atmosphere from Medellín as befits somewhere that calls itself the salsa capital of the world. For one thing it was much hotter and – although I could sense Bertica didn't approve – I wound down the windows to hear the sensuous salsa rhythms. Although Cali sprawls like any large modern city, the centre is comparatively small. It is very old – established in 1536, a few years after the collapse of the Incas to Pizarro, along the banks of the river, which seemed to be the equivalent of the Pasaje Junin, full of people

113

walking in the shade of exotic-looking trees. It still had the feel of a colonial town. The women of Cali are reputedly the most beautiful in Colombia, and certainly the girls were dressed with far more flair than I had seen in Medellín. Skirts in Medellín were longer than I had become used to in London but several inches shorter here.

Bertica's family lived in the area known as the Ciudad Jardin – the garden city – and this was rich man's land: the road leading to her house was patrolled by a uniformed watchman, complete with submachine-gun.

The house was similar to those I had seen in Medellín belonging to my clients – modern, large and airy – but this was the first time I had slept in one. My bedroom looked over the garden, which an army of workmen maintained as if it was Kew Gardens. There was air-conditioning and, naturally, I had my own bathroom. Later that afternoon I joined the children swimming in the indoor pool. There was also an outdoor pool, but by this time it was raining – one of the regular downpours that make Cali's climate so pleasant.

If this wasn't enough the family were determined to entertain their foreign visitor and the next day we set off for the family *finca*, a more low-key, rustic place. But it had its own private lake and a thirty-foot-high waterfall, which provided endless sport for the children, who would dare each other to run under it, and to Bertica's father, who stood under it at every opportunity letting the water splash over his beer belly of which he seemed inordinately proud.

At the side of the house was a corral, where six horses were tethered. Did I ride? Well, yes, I did. I didn't admit that I hadn't ridden for about seven years, since I was a student. Learning to ride had been part of the course. Sometimes the only way to diagnose a horse is to just get onto it. Also, horsy people have a problem with those they don't think 'one of us'. Being able to ride goes some way to dispelling the idea that they are dealing with an idiot.

I needn't have worried. My companions were Bertica's children Alejandro and Claudia who – although not yet four – was quite happy to sit behind Alejandro on his horse. But I didn't disgrace myself, and soon we had left the *finca* behind and were deep in the forest that covered the mountains.

The next day we were off again, this time to Silvia, the home of an unusual Indian community. It took several hours to reach, but – for me anyway – was worth it. Silvia lies high in a valley and the local people are Guambiano Indians, who were friendly and open. They looked different from the local people I had met the previous week in the north in their bright clothes of blue and shocking pink. All too soon it was time to return to Cali and one last dinner with Bertica's family.

At the clinic on my first day back I met up with Cristina, wondering what sort of Christmas she had had. I knew that things were tight financially – not for her the weekly migration to the *finca* in the country at weekends – but beyond that I had no idea how ordinary people lived.

She seemed cheerful enough and was busy arranging for me to go to Cúcuta to get my resident's visa. She had booked a ticket for me to fly the next day, she said. Still no sign of Eduardo. He had been back briefly, it seemed, and Maria told me she had heard him and Pilar rowing. She thought Eduardo had returned to Apartado.

My first morning back was comparatively easy – only two appointments. This was something of a relief because before Christmas I had decided that I had to supplement my earnings and that teaching English was the obvious answer. Besides, I needed something to do: reading the paper while

I waited for clients who might or might not turn up was deadly dull. I wasn't good at hanging around.

I had an interview in a language school that afternoon.

As if to confirm my decision, our nine o'clock appointment that morning turned up at eleven. Not bad, I reflected. At least it was the right day. It was another German shepherd, and it didn't take me long to reach a diagnosis. Nelly was a thin dog with twitching muscles, a crusty nose and something I hadn't seen for a long time: all her pads were thickened and cracking. Hard pad. This was a classic symptom for the tertiary stages of distemper, a very nasty disease. I had rarely seen it, although in the UK it was common apparently just after the Second World War, as Tony Self, my old boss at the Harmsworth, had told me.

'How long has she been ill?' I asked her owner, an old man – who I suspected was an employee of the true owner, who couldn't be bothered to come here himself.

This was confirmed when he said he wasn't sure. 'Maybe a few days?' he said, in a helpful way, seemingly plucking the possibilities out of the air as he studied the ceiling.

'A few days? A few months more like,' I told him. 'Has Nelly had any fits?'

A flash of illumination lit up the old man's wrinkled face. He took off his sun hat to reveal a corrugated bald head that wrinkled even further as he concentrated on remembering when Nelly had had her first fit.

I gave Cristina a help-me-please look. The only way I could improve my understanding was by working it out for myself but there were times when this was just a waste of time. Cristina took over and I listened to several minutes of rapid-fire Spanish.

The dog had been treated before. 'He says she has seen three veterinarians who all say a different thing. She may

116

have been ill for three months. His boss told him not to say anything about the other vets because he wanted the truth from the *inglés*.'

Ah, yes, an Englishman's word and all that. As I spoke to the old man I knew that in all probability I would never see poor Nelly again. For lack of a simple, inexpensive vaccine she was in the last stages of an illness that would probably kill her, and had caused untold suffering. 'There is nothing I can do for her except end her misery,' I said.

The old man's eyes lifted to heaven. This was news he wouldn't want to take back to his employer, who had clearly heard that the *inglés* was a miracle-worker.

'The dog has *moquillo*, distemper,' I told him, hoping that he might have heard of it.

The old man's face took on an expression of pleading. 'Will not an injection help?'

Belief in the magical power of an injection is not confined to Colombia, I thought ruefully. 'I will give her a multivitamin shot,' I said. Cristina nodded at this: I had forgotten that it was virtually impossible to get a fee unless you did something, even if you didn't believe it would do any good.

Nelly submitted to the injection and the old man paid a hundred pesos. I watched the man and the dog stagger out together, wondering what the next vet would diagnose.

Then I heard a familiar toot, and there were Pedro Ramirez, his elegant wife and a rejuvenated Bonita. She pulled a hideous expression, showing a magnificent set of teeth, as soon as I looked at her. She would need to be trussed up. She had evidently forgotten that she had spent a night curled up next to me.

Pedro had been told that when dogs had been ill they needed appetite stimulants in the form of an injection. He had brought her in for one. I didn't relish a fight with the dog, which might burst her stitches, but Pedro came into his role as owner by putting Bonita into a headlock that would have done justice to a Sumo wrestler. I was able to inspect the wound, which was healing beautifully, and administer another unnecessary multivitamin injection.

The real reason for the visit, however, was that Emma's favourite racehorse had performed badly a few days before, having been expected to win. Would I visit? I looked at Cristina. I had little experience of racehorses. Make that none. On the other hand, a one-off visit wouldn't do any harm. She nodded – I had to consider her wages too. 'Fine,' I agreed, 'but later this week. I have to go into town today and Cúcuta tomorrow. You can pick me up on Wednesday afternoon.'

Pedro extended his hand. 'Five hundred pesos?' he enquired.

'Pick me up earlier. Five hundred pesos plus lunch.'

Pedro laughed. 'You are becoming a true *paisa*,' he said.

Then I had a sudden thought. 'Although, if the *consulado* is its usual efficient self I may have to stay over in Cúcuta on Tuesday night.'

Pedro looked at me in amazement.

'You can pay a taxi driver a thousand pesos and he will drive you across the border, wait for you and drive you back. It is simple. Those sons-of-whores will be grateful for the money.'

I thought about this. 'Is it that easy?'

'Of course.' He snorted. 'Agree the price before you get in. Walk away if they try for any more money. They will come running, you will see.'

He grinned, shook hands and sped away with his wife and dog.

¡Viva El Vet!

With a couple of hundred pesos in my pocket I got the bus into town. I paid the one-peso fare and hung on for dear life. We made the centre in five minutes and two salsa melodies. I didn't need to hold on to any straps because I was pressed up against numerous bodies, with my hands firmly in my pockets clutching my money and my watch.

I had an interview at two o'clock with the owner of the Institute of Modern English, just across the way from where Gloria's parents lived. Maybe I could visit them afterwards. I hadn't heard from Gloria for a while but I had heard that she was going out with another Englishman.

I decided to take a walk in the centre of town to kill time and eat after the interview. I meandered up the Pasaje Junin, marvelling at the sheer variety of people, mostly young, pretty girls out for a walk in their lunch-hour. There were lots of comments made to the girls by all and sundry. These were known as '*piropos*', a kind of verbal wolf whistle and seemed to be routine and enjoyed by the girls. They could give as good as they got. As for '*bizcocho*' – even I was getting used to it and smiling at whoever had said it. Pretty harmless fun.

Then I walked across the Bolivar Park, pausing to listen to a brass band playing some light classical music. They were a little out of tune but somehow that seemed to make the sound all the more charming and they had to compete with the *gamines* yelling, 'Cigarillos Kenny Morlbro!'

In the corner of the square a badly dressed young man was hissing, '*Se vende*,' and every now and then he displayed what he was selling: a Yorkshire terrier puppy. He only brought it out when he spotted a possible punter; the rest of the time the pup was concealed in his jumper. It wouldn't have surprised me if it had belonged to one of my clients, and as I was thinking this, a well-dressed woman in her

119

thirties gave the man some money and walked off with the little dog. This seemed to be a universal system that belonged to all stolen items. Anything which couldn't be nailed down was up for grabs – windscreen wipers were a favourite, along with wristwatches, any jewellery and even spectacles. Rather than buy new versions of the stolen goods Colombians preferred to check out '*donde las ratas*' – or where the rats, in this case thieves, were to be found, and buy back the stolen goods, whatever they were, for a lower price than usual. Thus the system perpetuated itself.

When I neared the Metropolitan Cathedral I decided on impulse to go in. That was the first problem. It seemed half the *pordioseros* in town had congregated on its steps. Said to be the biggest cathedral in South America, it was a magnet for them. Camped on the steps were some of the most pitiful people I had seen yet: one young man had lost both arms and legs and was being towed around outside the cathedral by his friend on an improvised cart. He shouted, '*Por Dios*,' and I gave him a ten-peso note.

'May God pay you,' said his friend.

There were babies with kwashiorkor, their bloated stomachs exposed by their mothers for all to see, young children with rickets, swollen joints and knock-knees, hanging on to their mothers' skirts. Some of the older beggars – mostly women – had deformed hands and feet, which I found out later from some doctor friends was leprosy. Most of the beggars' skins were peeling due to nutritional deficiencies. From time to time a plump priest would emerge from the cathedral, his sleek, oily features in shocking contrast with what was all around him. I saw three or four step delicately over the beggars as though they did not exist with that peculiar grace that only the truly obese possess. I squeezed inside and found myself in the calm, peaceful environment universal in big churches. The pulpit was all marble and the opulent stained-glass windows let rays of light through, which settled on the heads of the devout praying silently in the pews.

I stayed for a while, trying to make sense of what I had seen outside, then steeled myself to leave, determined to give another ten-peso note to someone. I handed it to an old woman sitting by the door. Her legs were bloated and cracked – surely she couldn't live long in that state? She looked up at me, smiled a toothless smile, and tucked the note under her poncho.

Again I questioned what I was doing treating dogs and cats of the rich when all this poverty surrounded me. It was a question that haunted me more and more.

I was late for my appointment but realised it hardly mattered. This was Colombia, and when I arrived Alonso and his son Jairo were still at lunch. They eventually showed up at a quarter past three. Jairo was a cheerful extrovert, dressed casually in a multicoloured shirt and expensive jeans. A few years earlier he had made some money as a member of a pop group that had had a couple of hits. His father, now into his seventies, I guessed, was much more restrained in a light suit and, unusually, a tie. It didn't matter that I didn't have any experience: they wanted someone who spoke fluent English. The fact that I was from England scored heavily in my favour since the general consensus in Colombia was that the best English was spoken in England (little did they know), just as every Colombian thinks that the purest Spanish in South America is to be found in Colombia.

When I told Jairo that I was getting my working visa the next day, he said I could start next week, some afternoons from three until five and every evening from six until eight. I went back to one of the restaurants in Pasaje Junin and had the largest meal on the menu, washed down with a couple of beers. I could afford to eat like a king now. I wondered what teaching English would be like and whether I should give up being a vet for a while. Then I thought of Fidel and others like him – maybe part-time vet and part-time teacher would work.

I felt a little depressed, lonely and suddenly homesick as I listened to the strains of the band, who were still playing what sounded like Mozart. I missed London, the South Bank, the concerts, my friends, parents – everything. I clapped my hands loudly and ordered another beer. With my improved economic status I treated myself to a ride home in a *buseta* – a little bus, not much different from a single-decker at home – in which you were guaranteed a seat. No standing allowed.

The fare was 2 pesos – still nothing, but a measure of my need to economise that I hadn't used this form of transport until now. After a good night's sleep I felt better in the morning as I made my way to the airport, strangely reassured to see the faithful old Viscount on the runway ready to transport the usual motley bunch of travellers to Cúcuta.

The captain, probably in his fifties but looking older, greeted me as an old friend, even though this was only the third time I had flown with Aeropesca, and therefore hardly qualifying for frequent flier status. He showed off the cockpit with obvious pride in his plane. I told him I was hoping to make the trip back today and, out of the blue, he volunteered to negotiate with a taxi driver – he knew some from those occasions when he had to stop over due to a technical problem. We landed spot on time and the captain and I were last off. We got to the terminal building and in no time I was fixed up with a driver who for a thousand pesos, just as Pedro had said, would take me to the border and wait while my passport was stamped. I was over the border and at the Consulate in fifteen minutes, but my heart sank when I saw the queue.

The taxi driver, always smiling and with an honest face, turned out to have diplomatic skills too. The 'gringo' doctor was expected back in his hospital in Medellín tonight, could I be seen quickly?

The queue parted in deference to my status and the procedures were completed in an hour. The taxi driver took me to a pleasant open-air restaurant near the airport, and I was so pleased that I bought him a meal and a few beers to pass the time, and a bottle of *aguardiente* for the captain.

As usual the flight took off exactly on time. I settled down contentedly with my glass of orange juice and flicked through the pages of my passport. There it was on pages ten and eleven. The *visa ordinaria*. Lots of official writing, instructions to present myself to the police in Medellín within forty-eight hours and a couple of stamps that looked as if they would be worth something one day. But the visa was worth a lot to me right now. I could live in Colombia for the rest of my life, if I so pleased. For a few seconds I wondered what that would be like and dismissed it as fanciful. I knew that everything I enjoyed about Colombia would become oppressive if I didn't have England to go back to.

The stewardess interrupted me in my daydream. The captain had asked it I would like to sit in the cockpit for the descent into Medellín. It was an astounding sight, with the mountains towering above us on all sides and the city stretched before us.

The first officer, an absurdly young-looking man, was

piloting the plane. He looked up as I came in then got on with his job, occasionally responding to instructions from the captain. I handed over the bottle of *aguardiente* and said everything had gone to plan. On the last part of the descent both pilots were busy, and once again I couldn't believe how near we were to the centre of town. I picked out the clinic easily as we passed over it to land seconds later. As we touched down I heard a ripple of applause from the other passengers.

'They are content with the landing,' said the captain, with obvious pride. 'His first,' he added, indicating the young pilot with a nod. I saw a bead of sweat on his brow.

I left the plane with a tinge of regret – it was the only airline I had ever flown with that had a family atmosphere about it, and the in-flight entertainment was unbeatable. Going through the arrivals lounge I heard someone call my name and was surprised to see Ernst Schwarzkopf looking worried and relieved at the same time. 'Come vid me, Dr Grant,' he said propelling me towards the door. 'Bosun has a problem.'

He had called Cristina and she had told him the flight I was expected in on.

'The vet in Miami is standing by to take de evening flight if you didn't make it back today.'

He asked me to wait while he phoned home and presumably cancelled the Miami man. I had heard that Janina had flown her vet from Miami down for the day more than once when Bosun had a serious problem. My heart sank. What could the problem be? Could we cope with the basic facilities at our disposal? We jumped into Ernst's TR3 – handing over a wad of notes to the parking watchman who had stayed with the car while Ernst waited for me – and sped off.

Chapter 9

As we drove from the airport to the Schwarzkopfs' *finca* in the Poblado district, Ernst put me in the picture. Bosun had run round the garden at his usual speed that morning and somehow managed to collide with a tree. He had been found by one of the maids, semi-conscious and bleeding from his mouth. Janina had been out at the time and came back to find the dog pawing at his mouth and dripping blood.

I arrived to a house in high drama. Bosun was lounging on a sofa, all padded up with blankets. His mistress was weeping and a couple of the staff were in attendance, hovering, not sure what to do.

'Thank God you made it!' Janina said, as I hurried into the room. Bosun was so pleased to see me that he jumped off the sofa and bounced around me with his tail stump wagging furiously. Obviously he wasn't still in shock.

I patted his head and looked at his lips to try to see how much blood he might have lost. Not much, I concluded, although there was an impressive amount of blood on the blanket. I asked for a bowl of iced water and some cotton wool. Ernst barked orders and they appeared moments later on a silver tray.

I sat in front of Bosun and I gently opened his mouth. Two of his front incisor teeth were hanging off. I looked up at Janina, who was as pale as a ghost and wondered how to get her out of the room.

Ernst made the decision for me. 'Vait outside, my dear.

Dis vill be man's verk.' It seemed very old-world, the way he said it.

'Don't hurt him, please don't hurt him,' were his wife's last words, as she fled from the room.

I opened the boxer's mouth again and pushed a cotton-wool swab soaked in the cold water against the gum. He bit on it as if playing. It was enough to dislodge the two teeth, which fell out on to the carpet. A couple of minutes' pressure with the cotton wool was enough to stem any further bleeding. 'I reckon he'll be hungry after that,' I remarked. 'Let me feed him.' I wanted to make sure the dog realised who his friends were. I made him sit and wait, then ordered him to tuck into a large bowl of dog food. Janina came in as he was licking the remains out of the bowl. I showed her the two teeth. 'I expect he'll be getting a visit from the tooth fairy tonight.'

'Oh, my God, Bosun.' She smothered the dog with kisses. 'Will he need restorative dentistry?'

'Well, you can talk to the vet in Miami, if you like,' I replied, 'but it's not something I would recommend, or do. Dogs can manage very well without any teeth at all. As it is, he'll just have a gap at the front. Rather charming, I think.'

'Vat can I get you, Dr Grant? A visky, perhaps?'

Ernst had read my mind. What a day I had had. I needed to celebrate. 'Make it a large one,' I grinned, 'on the rocks.'

He joined me with a glass even bigger than mine and topped up both after half an hour. By now his wife had regained her composure and had changed into a light see-through dress, which left nothing to the imagination. Although she must have been about sixty she looked a lot younger, the result due less to nature's natural bounty than Ernst's capacious wallet.

I suddenly felt profoundly tired and was relieved but also

slightly alarmed when my host offered to drop me off at the clinic. He seemed to have the constitution of an ox, though, as his driving didn't seem any different even after two huge whiskies. The effect on me was more noticeable – I stammered out my thanks as he passed me twenty dollars. I slowly climbed up to my room. I'd just lie down for a few minutes.

At two in the morning I woke with my bladder bursting. In the street below I could hear guitars and a singer. Across the road, lights went on and windows opened to hear the songs. Whoever it was had a beautiful voice and the musicians could have been professionals. I suddenly realised they were singing outside Pilar's room, which was next to mine. I peered out and caught sight of who else but Hector; I thought I had heard that voice before.

It was a *serenata* for his girlfriend. Poor Eduardo, he didn't stand a chance, I thought. I had heard that *serenatas* were popular as a means of showing your love and devotion, and that every girl expected one during a courtship. There were bands in the centre of town, who for a small consideration would come and play, normally six songs, outside your girlfriend's window. Traditionally this should be at dead of night. The girlfriend would switch her light on and off to signal that she had heard the songs, and the suitor would then slip a note under her door to say who they were from. All very romantic.

What amazed me was that everyone woke up to enjoy the entertainment – no phoning of the police for causing a disturbance or shouting abuse, as would likely have happened in London. Pilar went a step further and invited everyone in. I heard her calling out to Maria, ordering coffee for everyone.

An impromptu party started downstairs but I had not the remotest wish to join in. In fact, after a much-needed trip to the loo, I was soon dead to the world again. I had things to do tomorrow: a look at Emma Ramirez' horse in the morning and a trip to the dreaded DAS – the immigration and plain-clothes police – in the afternoon. I had to arrange my *cédula* – the identification document that every Colombian is required to carry at all times. I had been warned never to venture out without some form of ID. If I was picked up in any of the frequent sweeps by the police following any disturbances I would be fined fifty pesos and risk a night in clink if I didn't have it with me.

Amazingly, the lovely Emma was at the clinic first thing, looking even more glamorous than usual in immaculate jodhpurs and boots that must have cost a fortune. I hadn't forgotten about the horse, had I? I explained that I wasn't an equine specialist, but she said that didn't matter. And part of me was intrigued. They were such a strange couple, I wondered how they lived. No one else had turned up at the clinic so I jumped into the jeep and sped off to the Poblado district. Inevitable, really, that they would live in the poshest part of town.

It really was a different planet. Emma and Pedro lived not far from Ernst and Janina Schwarzkopf. We passed the turning to the estate where they lived. I hadn't heard any more about Bosun, so presumed he was back to normal. It suddenly occurred to me, economics never having been my strong point, that twenty dollars was a huge saving on the airfare from Miami plus the fees for the American vet's professional services that Janina would have had to pay if I hadn't turned up.

I dismissed such an ungenerous thought from my mind as we swung into the ranch where Emma lived. I was getting used to this opulence: a huge *Dallas*-style farmhouse, horses in the paddocks, the inevitable swimming pool, and beautiful views of the mountains. All this came at a price and there was heavy security everywhere. The source of the wealth I found out later was bananas. Pedro owned thousands of plantations to the north, which he would visit from time to time in his private plane. There was a small airstrip in sight of the farmhouse. Emma's hobby was horses. They seemed happy enough, but unusually for a Colombian couple, they didn't have children.

The horse was brought out for my inspection. The trainer, who was originally from Cartagena on the Caribbean coast, gabbled away as to what he thought the problem was but all I could pick up were vitamins and poor appetite. Later Pedro chuckled at my difficulty: the *costeños*, as people from the coastal regions were called, were impossible for a gringo to understand.

I asked Emma some questions and used her as my interpreter. The horse was a four-year-old bay called Rocky. It had shown great promise in training but had broken down in its last race just a week ago and had not run well in training since. I thanked my horse lecturer at college as I began to look at the animal. His lectures had been superb and at least I knew how to examine this fine specimen properly. I went over him from head to tail. He seemed to be breathing a bit fast. I asked the trainer to trot him up. He did so, and on exertion there was a soft cough. With the horse sweating slightly I repeated my examination. There was no doubt about it – there was crackling in the chest now. Further questions elicited that the horse had had the cough, along with several others, but it had been put down to a dusty stable.

All in all I spent an hour on the case and then we went to look at the drugs available in the stable area. It was quite usual in Colombia for horse-owners to keep a supply of their own drugs, as they do in England. Even so, the collection surprised me: half a dozen antibiotics, drenches of every description, and an impressive array of needles and syringes. There were no legal restrictions about what could be kept on hand.

Although I had gone equipped only with a thermometer and a stethoscope, and had warned them that I wasn't a specialist in horse practice, I had carried out a thorough examination and I felt sure enough of my diagnosis to give an opinion. It looked as though there had been an outbreak of respiratory virus in the stables. Rest and recuperation were necessary. I explained that because the cough was most probably caused by a virus, no drugs would help, just good nursing – and, of course, it would be madness for the horse to race when suffering from a viral infection. Not only would he lose, but his lungs might be damaged permanently too.

I wasn't sure if my advice would be heeded, but on seeing a multivitamin injection on the shelf I loaded the syringe and injected the stallion in the pectoral muscle. 'This will make the muscle sore for two weeks. Do not run the horse for two weeks.' A simple message. The 'power' of the injection plus the two weeks' enforced rest should do the trick. It was time for lunch.

Sitting by the pool, *al fresco*, with the gardens and mountains all around us seemed utterly unreal. Earlier when I had arrived the grounds had been filled with gardeners and people whose job seemed to be to rake the gravel. Now there was no one. Like their bosses, they were having lunch, which lasted at least two hours.

Only two days before I had been feeling homesick for England, and now all that seemed to fade into insignificance. I explained that although I was happy to see to Rocky I didn't intend to take up horse work seriously. 'For one thing,' I explained, as Pedro pressed me, 'the clinic here doesn't have any equipment to deal with horses. What happens if one needs an operation?'

Pedro replied that they sometimes flew in a vet from Manizales, a town not too far away – maybe half an hour in his plane – or in extreme circumstances they would get an American in. It seemed that Janina Schwarzkopf wasn't the only one to go to these lengths. Pedro fondled his wife's arm. 'Anything to keep this woman happy.'

I mentioned Jaime Ochoa in Envigado and how he also wanted me to look at his horses. A look of alarm flashed across both Emma and Pedro's faces. 'If I were you I would make yourself unavailable,' Pedro said. It was the first time I had seen him without a smile on his lips, but he wouldn't elaborate except to say, looking nervously over his shoulder as if there were eavesdroppers, '*Mala gente*' – bad people. He tapped his nose and made a throat-slitting gesture. He wasn't joking.

We sat down for lunch. They certainly ate healthily: we had chicken, rice and salad, with some delicious tropical juice to drink. Just right, and I had to tear myself away all too quickly. 'I have to visit DAS in Medellín to sort out my *cedula*,' I explained. 'My appointment is at two.'

Pedro looked at his watch. 'But it is only one-thirty.' he said, looking confused.

'It will take me half an hour to get there.'

'But this is Medellín. You don't have to get there on time.'

I explained that, where my visa was concerned, I was intending to stick to English time. This was the last part of the elaborate rigmarole to allow me to stay indefinitely – if I wanted.

As I waited for Pedro to get the car – he had decided to take me himself – I gazed at the mountains, the swimming pool, the gardens, and wondered if I could live like this.

'No,' I said to myself aloud. 'I couldn't.' It was strange: after months of effort to get a permanent visa, when I got it homesickness came almost instantly.

In town the secretary at the DAS office took five minutes to register my presence – she was busy on the phone, presumably talking to her boyfriend. She was quite striking in a typical Latin-American way: very dark, perfect skin, dark flashing eyes and an aggressively red lipstick plastered on. She had the amazing ability to smoke, talk and chew gum all at the same time. Eventually I got her attention and gave her my passport, which said on the visa, 'Present yourself to DAS in Medellín within 48 hours.' She took it and came back after five minutes, said, 'Photos,' and held out her hand.

'Photos?'

'You need photos for your *cédula*.' When she realised I didn't have any she indicated a shop opposite. 'Ask for Luís – he will do them. Twenty pesos.'

I did as I was asked. Luís was meticulous. Ten photos were taken of my face – from the side, front and every angle in between. Luís had a developing facility on site and an hour later I was back in front of the secretary. She looked at the photos and smiled. 'Very ugly,' she said, pausing mid-chew to look at one of the side shots, which I had to admit was not the most flattering picture ever taken of me.

She pulled out a three-page form that she began to fill in. The authorities wanted to know the names of my father, mother, sister, and my mother's maiden name. And that was just the starter for ten. Address, phone number, business phone number, date of birth, parents' date of birth, etc, etc. Then she looked carefully at my nose, ears, eyes, eyebrows and mouth, all the time making notes on the form. Finally, after about an hour of this, it was time to take my fingerprints. All digits on both hands five times.

¡Viva El Vet!

'So, you are a veterinarian?' she said.

'Yes, but I also plan to teach English while I am here,' I replied. The young woman with the slash of red lipstick considered this. A large bubble appeared from her mouth, while smoke came down both nostrils. The bubble burst and she added, 'I have always wanted to learn English. I will phone you for some private lessons. My name is Blanca. This is your phone number?'

I nodded.

'So I phone. OK?'

As we were talking, a succession of petty delinquents had been coming and going with police agents, both uniformed and in plain clothes, while my form-filling was going on. There was an air of menace about the place. I didn't feel I could refuse any request here.

'Why not? It's a useful language,' I replied.

'And the English from England is the most perfect English – no?'

I couldn't disagree, but my attention was distracted by two *gamines*, arrested for stealing a handbag, caught in the act by a vigilant plain-clothes DAS agent. He made them stand in front of Blanca and gave one a hefty cuff at the back of his head when he wouldn't stand up straight. Blanca gave them both an icy stare and demanded their names and ages. Both boys were fourteen. I was staggered.

'Fourteen?' I blurted out. They looked about eight. And a small eight at that.

'These ruffians always look younger. Years of living on the street stunt them. Mind and body,' said Blanca, speaking in a hard, colloquial Spanish. All sweetness and interest had gone. It was clear what her solution would be: lock them up and throw away the key – or worse. She made a note of their details and left them with the policeman to process. I wondered what their future would be. Bleak would be putting it mildly.

'Don't worry about them,' Blanca said, aware of my silence. 'Medellín has too many of them. Those two won't be causing any further trouble.' She blew a bubble provocatively, looking straight into my eyes. 'Your identification document will be ready in ten weeks, but I hope to see you before that.' She added, in English, 'Goodbye,' although it came out as Hoodbye. I never saw her again.

By now it was four in the afternoon. I made a phone call to Cristina at the clinic. No work had come in, but two vaccinations were booked for tomorrow. Easy money, and I felt a bit relieved. My own prospects might have taken a turn for the better but I still had Cristina's wages to think of. I decided to go up to the Institute of Modern English to make myself known to the other teachers – soon to be colleagues and, I hoped, friends.

'David!' I turned to see Jairo coming towards me with a young girl, one of his students, no doubt. 'I wasn't expecting you today.'

'I've been down at the DAS getting my mug shots,' I explained, 'so I just thought I'd come and say hello.'

'Mug shots?'

'Photographs – for the *cédula*. It's a term used when there's no attempt at artistry. Just for identification, usually for criminals. Mug is a slang word for face.'

'And you were worried about being a novice. You're a teacher already and I can see it's not just the students who'll be learning from you.'

We walked out on to the veranda that fronted the school from where you could look out on to the street. It was used as a general meeting place and was where people went when they had a break. I was introduced to some of the teachers, who were drinking coffee. They were two Americans both younger than me. Tom was an extrovert twenty-two-year-old from Philadelphia. He was tall and boasted a shock of red hair and a moustache that would have done credit to Che Guevara. He jumped up and shook my hand as if I was a long-lost friend. He oozed charm. He had half the women in town after him, so I was told, and I could believe it. When I was with him and a pretty girl called out, '*Bizcocho*,' I knew it wasn't for me. He spoke quickly and jumped from one idea to another all the time. He was heavily into Colombian politics and the Medellín way of life, having absorbed the local accent with hardly a trace of American. Later, I found out that he had selected Medellín to live based on his certainty that nuclear war with Russia was inevitable and that they would leave South America alone. He thought that the altitude would also make Medellín somehow safer, although I couldn't see how. Then there was Dan, a quiet Texan. Dan was deeply religious and had turned to teaching to make ends meet while he devoted the rest of his energies to converting Colombians from their Catholicism to his sect's form of Protestantism. Shortly after I arrived he got up to take a class.

'Mind if David sits in, Dan?' said Jairo, as Dan collected his students' papers. 'He needs to see how we do this.'

The school was proud to have written its own textbook and students learned by chanting sentences from it. Dan's class had reached negatives and I heard them chant in unison, 'Are there saints in the church? No, there aren't saints in the church,' and so on. It didn't seem very inspiring but the students seemed to be happy enough.

There were twenty in each class and virtually all were girls, secretaries mainly, and none older than their early

135

twenties. Two other teachers, both Colombians who had lived for some time in the USA, made up the teaching staff, and I met them in the canteen after Dan's class was over.

There was Freddy, a small man with long curly hair with a New York accent, and Ramón, who looked like a Cherokee Indian and spoke like a New York taxi driver. 'You wanna go have a beer?' he asked me, after I left Dan to go off to his next class. A beer sounded good to me.

We had only got as far as the Edificio Coltejer (the Ave Maria Building), when we were both stopped by a soldier. His uniform marked him out as a private and he had the features of a *campesino*. There were other soldiers similarly engaged. I was made to stand against the wall with both hands resting on it and my legs spreadeagled. Rather than ask me to stand that way, the soldier kicked my legs apart, and I was roughly frisked. Ramón asked him what was going on. I couldn't understand a word that passed between them. 'Apparently there has been an assassination of some important lawyer half an hour ago, right here in the centre,' explained Ramón laconically, as though it was an everyday occurrence.

Two youths, with crash helmets, on a motorcycle had stopped beside the victim while he sat in his car at the traffic lights and shot him. The response had been to swamp the centre with police and troops in a major sweep. The private was not satisfied with my passport.

'Where's your *cédula*?' Ramón asked. I explained that it was ten weeks away. Ramón spoke to the soldier, who wavered but wouldn't make any decision without passing it through an officer. Fortunately Ramón attracted the attention of the officer in charge, who turned out to be reasonable. I was freed after fifteen anxious minutes.

'You were lucky,' said Ramón. 'You might have been arrested and they take a long time to ask questions. In the meantime you'd be stuck with those.' He gestured with his thumb to a villainous-looking bunch of hard men sitting on the floor, guarded by a young soldier with a machine-gun, with their hands on their heads. Every now and then one would get a kick, as a reminder to keep still and keep his hands on his head.

By now we were up in the bar overlooking Pasaje Junin. Stop-and-searches were still going on but we were safe here for the time being. 'If they decide on a curfew we'll have to get the hell out of town,' my companion said, with a grin. He had lit up an American cigarette, one of the Kents that were constantly being hawked by *gamines*. Sitting there, the cigarette at the side of his mouth, his eyes screwing up whenever he drew on it, he looked and sounded exactly like an American gangster.

He explained that whenever there was big trouble, a riot or a prominent murder, the word would go out – get off the streets. Anyone found out and about during a curfew would be slung into the bullring for the night and questions asked the next day. Like all towns with a Spanish past, Medellín had its bullring. To spend the night in this way was a fate almost worse than death since most of the town's petty criminals would be in the same place and a gringo would be looked upon as a legitimate, easy target. And there would be no protection or sympathy from the police. I clapped my hands and ordered another couple of beers and something to eat. Might as well sit it out in comfort while things cooled down. Ramón told me something about himself.

His parents had taken him to New York when he was three and he had been educated there until he was sixteen when his parents had separated. His mother had come back to Medellín with him and he had had to find work to support them both. He had been lucky to get work in a factory making suits. He was still there, making enough to eat and supplementing it with teaching late afternoons and evenings. He didn't have a regular girlfriend – not enough money. 'What I need right now,' he said, 'is a piece of tail.' This was one of Ramón's favourite phrases to describe a prospective amorous encounter. His eyes lit up at the thought and to emphasise the point he nodded with glee at two women below, who had decided that this was a good moment to ply their trade. They made a comical but sad sight with their skirts hitched way up and low cut blouses. Both were well past their prime and not having much success. For a horrible moment, I thought that Ramón was going to invite them up. He would only have had to nod. But he was in full stride, describing the kind of woman he hoped eventually to marry. Very Catholic, pure, dedicated to him and pleased with his virility if from time to time he succumbed to temptation and chased 'a piece of tail'.

I got back to the clinic without further adventures. Maria made me coffee and I played with her son, who was just now starting to crawl. Pilar was out with Hector, so it seemed.

I had not spent much time talking to Maria. When Pilar was around she was like a mouse. I found out that she had not left the house for ten days over Christmas. Pilar had got in enough food and instructed Maria not to go out under any circumstances. With the constant stream of people knocking at the door for money it would have been only a matter of hours before the house was burgled. I felt sorry for Maria but she seemed quite happy to have spent her days looking after her son without having to work. I had to admit he was a cute little boy, who smiled and begged to be picked up whenever he saw me.

¡Viva El Vet!

The only problem with having two jobs in Colombia was timing. I could make an appointment in the morning to ensure that I was free to teach in the afternoon, but would the patient turn up? Miracle of miracles – the next day our vaccinations turned up on time. Both clients had nice little puppies. Cristina busied herself typing out prescriptions for wormers, vitamins and minerals and advising on diet. Each consultation took three-quarters of an hour, a far cry from the minutes involved in the same thing at home, but the clients insisted on their pound of flesh, wanting to know every conceivable thing about the rearing of puppies. They certainly got good service for their money. Cristina had just cashed up when there was another ring at the door. She came back looking agitated, her eyes widely dilated with fear. She indicated behind her, just able to say, 'DAS', as two swarthy men with very dark sunglasses came in with her.

'You are Dr Grant?' one asked. I nodded. I wasn't going to quibble about my title at this point. Surely they couldn't think I had anything to do with the assassination attempt? I should have felt terrified, but I felt as if I was in a *Monty Python* sketch. Both men were in uniform. They were small, up to my shoulder, with moustaches, and the dark glasses. Both their jackets had bulges in them, which I took to be guns. They were polite but unsmiling. 'Passport.'

I told them it was upstairs. The junior one came with me. When we returned, the senior put his hand on my shoulder. 'Dr Grant. You are under arrest. You must come with us now.'

I looked at Cristina in puzzlement. She was flicking her wrist, which she always did when she was frightened. I shrugged my shoulders, deciding to say nothing while I was led away to the policemen's open jeep and put inside.

139

Chapter 10

Sitting in the back of an open jeep was a funny way to be under arrest. The two policemen took it easy going into town, as if half hoping that I would try to jump ship. I had no such intentions, though: I had been here long enough to know that, for all my sprinting prowess, I wouldn't get five yards.

The two said nothing to me but instead engaged in rapid-fire jokes and comments about any woman who happened to be in view. What could it be about? I had already decided that it had nothing to do with the assassination: they'd have frisked me at least, and pulled the clinic to pieces searching for a gun. Surely my papers were in order? Blanca, the girl at the DAS office, had spent a good hour with all the documents. It must be a mistake. But it was to the DAS office that we went.

I was taken in under escort, a goon at each elbow, and left in a room with two other men and an armed guard at the door. No explanations – I just had to wait, apparently. No sign of Blanca: we'd taken another door from the main hall. I could have done with the sight of her cheery face, even though she was always chewing gum. Both my fellow detainees looked desperate.

I recognised one. He was the madman who entertained crowds on the Pasaje Junin or sometimes in the Bolivar Park. He was dressed in rags and had long hair, like some biblical character. He was filthy and gave off a pungent odour. He specialised in political satire, talking into an imaginary phone, as though he was in contact with various important people in the country. What he said about each person was apparently scandalous and he could often be seen giving these one-man shows surrounded by fifty or more spectators. If he succeeded in making them laugh enough he would collect a peso from each. At other times he would wander up and down shouting unintelligibly into the air. He was staring wildly now but fortunately paid no attention to me.

The other man sat in a dejected way on the floor paying no heed to anyone. After about an hour a well-dressed official in a suit came in and simply said to me, 'Passport,' holding out his hand.

I handed it over and decided to sit down on the floor in the corner. I had got used to the smell and was beginning to feel angry and frustrated. However, I knew better than to cause a rumpus: it would only make matters worse. The madman was bustled out after another twenty minutes, pushed in the back. Goodness knows what was in store for him.

It was my turn next. I was asked by the guard to follow him to the chief of police's office. And then it was back to *Monty Python*. The chief, a middle-aged man with a Saddam Hussein-type moustache, greeted me with a broad smile and actually shook my hand. 'I am sorry for this misunderstanding,' he said. 'You were reported by some . . . colleagues,' he paused over the word as if they clearly did not justify the name, 'for working without a permit. But I can see that your papers are perfectly in order'. He picked up my passport from his desk, handed it to me and shook hands again. 'You may go.'

I stumbled out into the warm sunshine, relieved that I hadn't been picked up last week, and decided to take a taxi back to the clinic where I knew that Cristina would be in a terrible state.

I arrived at the same time as a dapper middle-aged man with a Pekinese under his arm. Cristina let both of us in at the same time. Her relief was almost palpable but I didn't have time to explain as she recognised the client. She sat him down and got the details of the dog from the clinic records. Eduardo was enormously proud of his clinical records and he kept them for years, every now and then going through them and making notes, constantly trying to learn from his mistakes and triumphs.

'He is Fernando Echavarria,' said Cristina, while I cleaned the operating table before having a look at the patient. 'He is a superior judge. His brother is the governor of Antioquia,' she added reverently.

'I could have done with him two hours ago,' I muttered. She looked at me quizzically. 'I'll explain later.' Then she showed him in.

Fernando Echavarria looked about forty and was smartly dressed. He didn't fit my profile of a judge, let alone a superior judge, whatever that meant. He opened the proceedings in fluent English. His studies had included time at Oxford University, I later found out. As it was he introduced himself as 'a friend of Don Enrique Ruiz and his family. They said you might be able to sort out Poppy, who's the apple of my wife's eye. I've had to leave her at home. She just couldn't face it.'

He deposited Poppy gently on the stainless-steel operation-cum-consulting room table. I asked him, in true Anglo fashion, what seemed to be the trouble.

'Now, let me see,' he said, and fished out a note from his pocket. Taking a pair of half-moon glasses from another pocket he read out what his wife had written. 'Vomiting two days, drinking a lot of water, absolutely refuses to eat anything . . . let me see, yes, for a week. And there's a funny smell about her, especially at the back end.' He looked up at me, taking his glasses off. 'Ring any bells?'

'It does rather,' I said, with a worried frown. 'Let me have a look at her.' It didn't take long to confirm what I already knew. 'How old is she?'

'That I can tell you. She'll be eight this summer. We brought her back from England after I had finished my studies there.'

I prodded the little dog's abdomen. Not much doubt about it: I could feel a doughy mass occupying most of the available space. Poppy had a womb full of pus – a disease called pyometra. I had operated on countless such cases at the Harmsworth but always with the benefit of anaesthetic machines and twenty-four-hour nursing care afterwards. I told the judge my diagnosis and what would need to be done. I would have to remove the womb, a hysterectomy. 'You mean you can operate?' Clearly he hadn't anticipated this. 'Excellent news. My wife wasn't expecting to see the dog again.'

'Well,' I replied guardedly, 'I can't guarantee anything. The odds are only fifty-fifty that she makes it.'

I thought privately that the odds would be rather less than that. I would have only a simple batch of instruments at my disposal, a syringe of thiopentone, and that was that. No time to go down to the local hospital and get a bag of fluid. It would be surgery now and as quickly as possible. I told Fernando to go home and come back in an hour or so and we would see what could be done.

In this situation Cristina was as good as you could get. She set up the instruments and clipped up the operating site while Poppy was still conscious, to save time. The dog was so ill that she allowed herself to be laid on her back and cleaned up ready for surgery before we gave her the anaesthetic.

One of my big worries was her ability to breathe during the operation on her back, with the flat, crowded face that Pekinese have. Then I hit on the idea of using a couple of straws as a make-do airway. Cristina found some in the cupboard in the living room. We were ready. Just 1 cc of thiopentone was all it took to render Poppy unconscious, and I quickly put the two straws into her windpipe via her mouth so that the airway couldn't be obstructed.

Half an hour later an enormously distended womb was lying beside the dog on the operating table as I finished up stitching.

'Eh, *ave Maria*,' said Cristina, as the operation finished.

'We only perform miracles, here,' I said, with a grin. I looked at my watch – five o'clock in the afternoon. 'See if you can get hold of Dr Echavarria,' I said, giving him his inevitable title, 'and tell him to bring Poppy's bed here.'

Cristina frowned at this. 'Pilar will not like a dog staying overnight, especially if it whines,' she said.

'Don't worry, she won't know. The dog will spend the night with me.'

Cristina gave me a now-I-know-he's-mad look, but did as she was asked. I hadn't told her about my night with Bonita.

Dr Echavarria's wife answered the phone fully expecting bad news and her scream of delight could be heard over the phone in the operating theatre.

'Tell her it's not over yet,' I said. For one thing I hadn't yet removed the straws as breathing problems might result. And would the kidneys hold out? There was also the risk of peritonitis. Conditions were hardly sterile. Dozens of things might go wrong.

¡Viva El Vet!

Yet as I looked at the diminutive dog on the operating table I somehow felt that this one would be all right. It's curious how sometimes we go through a patch in life when everything turns out for the best. It was pure luck that the inefficient DAS had waited a couple of weeks before feeling my collar, and within the last couple of days I had done two big operations that looked as if they would turn out fine against the odds.

While we were making Poppy comfortable I filled in Cristina on the day's excitement. 'Hypocrites,' she said, referring to the vets who had tried to get rid of me. 'They were all smiles a few months back. You are "stealing" their business, I suppose.'

She was probably right. It seemed that few of the local vets were comfortable with anything more than minor surgery. This left a niche which I was starting to occupy, although with the somewhat limited facilities at my disposal it was not a niche in which I was particularly happy. And there were my doubts, too, as to whether my work was appropriate in this country. Teaching was beginning to look like a more attractive option and would be a good deal less stressful.

Señora Echavarria arrived with a large basket of soft cushions and smothered her half-conscious dog with kisses. 'I am so, so grateful,' she said, in English almost as good as her husband's. 'To be totally honest with you, Dr Grant, I hadn't expected to see Poppy alive again.' And with this thought she broke down in tears again and left us to it, promising to come in at nine the next morning.

The next problem was to find somewhere to keep Poppy out of Pilar's way. She had got into the habit of going out most evenings – presumably with lover-boy – after Maria had prepared some food. Cristina explained the situation to

145

Maria and we decided to tuck the dog in its basket in her room. This was one area pretty much guaranteed to be safe, as Pilar never went near it – the prospect of having to deal with Maria's little boy fazed her. In fact, he was already asleep. I looked down at him and felt sudden pity for the little fellow. No father – he had disappeared, as soon as he knew that Maria was pregnant. What would his future hold? I saw some elementary reading books by the side of his bed. 'A bit early for him?' I said, with a smile, touched by his mother's enthusiasm to ensure that he got an education.

'Oh, no,' Maria said blushing. 'They are for me. I am learning to read. Cristina is teaching me,' she added shyly.

I felt shame that Cristina, who had little enough time to spare and virtually no money, could find the time and probably the money to buy these meagre books when I was doing nothing. But now wasn't the moment to think over what I could do to help – I was shattered after all the excitement of the day. When Pilar was safely out of the way I had a shower as usual, collected Poppy from Maria's room at the back and carried her upstairs in her basket to my bedroom and turned in. Occasionally she snored or made retching sounds, which woke me instantly like a mother with her newly born baby. From time to time I offered the Peke sips of water and turned her over.

By eight o'clock in the morning Poppy was fully conscious if a bit doddery on her legs. She would make it, I decided, with a feeling of quiet triumph.

I showered quickly. (I had adopted Colombian customs, twice-daily showers being the norm.) Then, with Poppy safely under my arm, I crept downstairs. Pilar was waiting for me at the bottom, her mouth, never her most attractive feature, twisted in rage. 'What is that thing doing here?'

'This dog has been very ill, but she's going home in

an hour,' I replied wearily, not in the mood for an argument.

Pilar was not in a mood to be conciliatory and she launched into a tirade about how this was a house not a dog kennel. Maria came out, wondering what all the fuss was about, and got a tongue-lashing herself. I could take Pilar's abuse, but Maria was another matter. 'It's nothing whatsoever to do with Maria,' I said, suddenly aware that she might lose her job on my account – particularly if Pilar found out that the Peke had spent the previous evening in Maria's room. 'She knew nothing about it.'

A wave of anger rushed to my head at this arrogant woman. If the truth be known, I had probably been spoiling for a fight. Things had been simmering. For one thing her exploitation of the maid was nothing short of slavery. This was the first thing I felt needed to be pointed out. Second, there was the matter of the phone in the clinic: Pilar and her entire family were using it as their private line. While I remained here and in charge this would stop. The rest degenerated into a shouting match with Pilar storming out just as Cristina arrived.

Furious, I went upstairs to my room and brought down a small padlock, which had served as a lock on my hold-all. It fitted the phone perfectly. 'Only official phone calls from now on,' I told Cristina, giving her one of the keys and, pocketing the other.

'But she will go to Hector,' said Cristina, shaking her hand. 'This will mean trouble for you,'

'I don't care,' I replied. 'I have just about had enough of her. Eduardo's well out of it.'

For the first time I decided that, far from having drawn the short straw, Eduardo was well and truly better off now. And if the worst came to the worst I had a return ticket to England, valid for one year, locked away upstairs. I was tempted to use it – although that would feel like quitting after only four months. I needed a period of consolidation without all these dramas, a routine and a bit of fun too, I thought. I had been living a monkish life since I had arrived. Maybe the row would signal the start of better things to come.

Fernando Echavarria and his wife Victoria arrived at dead on nine. He looked at his watch and said proudly, 'English time,' and we laughed. Cristina busied herself with all the post-operative instructions and prescriptions for antibiotics while Victoria cradled her 'baby' in her arms. As soon as she saw her owners Poppy picked up enormously.

'Do you play golf, old chap?' Fernando said, after he had settled the bill with Cristina.

I grinned. 'I'm afraid I've only hit a few balls on a golf range.'

'So you're an expert then.' He laughed at his own joke. 'Don Enrique, Gustavo and I are having a round at the Club Campestre on Saturday. Perhaps you would care to join us.'

Cristina's eyes had lit up at the sound of the club, reputed, she later told me with great excitement, to be the last word in luxury. For a moment I contemplated asking if she could come with me, but chickened out. She would feel out of place in the company of the judge, affable chap though he was.

'Thank you very much. It'll be a pleasure,' I said. 'Maybe I can check out Poppy before we go.'

So it was settled. I was in for a bit of luxury this weekend and, no doubt, some good food. Much as I loved it, the bean stew was beginning to pall.

'He will be a good *palanca*,' said Cristina, as they left. 'And if Hector starts causing you trouble, believe me, you will need him.'

¡Viva El Vet!

She was right. Friends in high places might have spared me a couple of hours in the DAS cells yesterday. If influential enough, the *palanca* could sort out virtually anything.

I read the paper for an hour and dozed off before waking to see that it was two o'clock. There was nothing doing so I headed off into town for my first day as a teacher. The building was quite large with six classrooms, which could take up to thirty students each, and then there was the open-air veranda overlooking the street, where everybody went for coffee-breaks.

I arrived to see one of the street urchins Tom had befriended standing in the road shouting American swear words over and over again. All was explained when I went on to the veranda: Tom was leaning over the wrought-iron railings improving the boy's pronunciation and teaching him new swear words. Several *gamines* hung out around the school, mainly because Dan and some of the others gave them bits of food and sometimes change. That this boy, who was about fifteen, was being taught to swear elicited Dan's disapproval. When the boy got the pronunciation just right, Tom threw him a peso.

In the end Dan prevailed and Tom sat down and chatted, while a succession of pretty young girls flirted with him. He was incredible. He had somehow contrived for one of them to do his washing and ironing, which she delivered to him as we spoke. She was rewarded with a kiss but no money changed hands. Like everyone else, he lived a hand-to-mouth existence, but seemed happy enough. He bought a beer from the small bar attached to the lounge. Immediately one of the girls opened it and poured it for him. I wasn't sure if I should drink before a lesson so I started with a *tinto*.

The lessons were simple enough. I started by explaining

slowly who I was and asked people to read aloud from their set book, correcting the pronunciation as we went along. The main lesson *I* learned that first afternoon was that their book system was exceptionally boring, so after that I ignored it when I could, introduced new vocabulary, made up sentences and generally talked in English. No one complained and my students did as well, if not better, than the other teachers' students. It was strange: even though I was about as novice a teacher as you can imagine, I felt more comfortable in this role than I did dealing with pampered pets.

The time passed much more quickly than I had expected, and before I knew it, four hours and separate classes had gone. Time for some bean stew and beer. If everything continued to go to smoothly I shouldn't have any problems with my dual existence. As a routine it seemed tailor made: morning surgery, house visits or consultations in the early afternoon, followed by late afternoon and evening at the language school, then eating out and socialising.

Food in the ordinary restaurants was unbelievably cheap and it was hardly worth my while to go home. But it was a long day: I was working from nine in the morning until eight at night, albeit never under pressure. The most stressful part was keeping out of Pilar's way. If I could educate the clients to come during mornings only – and preferably 'English time' – it would be a sustainable routine. I wouldn't be making a fortune but neither would I be on the bread-line. Life felt a lot better, *and* there was the weekend to look forward to. If I could stretch it to a couple of years, then my Spanish would be pretty fluent.

'Your watch, David, mind your watch.' Ramón and I were on a bus going back to our respective neighbourhoods and his shout in English had the desired effect. I narrowly prevented the theft of my watch. I had managed to find a seat in the bus by the window and Ramón had spotted a boy reaching up from the pavement to wrench it off my wrist. In the nick of time I snatched my arm in, but the boy's nails scratched me. No one else commented.

Ramón had adopted English as our language of communication right from the start. 'How many times do I have to tell you, gringo? Keep your hands in your pockets in these buses,' he warned me. He had stationed himself at the back door and given himself the unofficial role of shouting to the driver when everyone had clambered on at each stop. It also gave him a vantage-point to see any villains and a quick escape route if any serious robbery occurred. I learned these street ways for myself under his tuition and they stood me in good stead.

'Beer Sunday night?' he said, as I got off near the clinic.

'Right. Pasaje Junin at eight – *de acuerdo*?' Done. It was time to see a bit more of Medellín at night.

I tiptoed in – but no sign of life, except for Maria and her still-unnamed son. I talked to her for a while before heading upstairs to write a few letters home. For a change they wouldn't be nostalgic ones.

Chapter 11

Saturday morning came and after breakfast of scrambled egg and *arepas*, faithfully prepared by Maria, I settled down with coffee and the paper. I found I could read most of it by now. There was an editorial complaining about the absence of security on the streets, with an increase in muggings and burglary. What were the authorities planning to do about it?

I didn't envy them their job. Crime was institutionalised in every aspect of Colombian society. I suddenly felt more than a little sorry for the Saddam Hussein lookalike at police headquarters, who was supposedly trying to stem the tide of violence. The seriously rich had massive security to shield them and only had to worry about kidnapping. It was ordinary people who suffered most. Thinking about the seriously rich heralded the arrival of Pedro Ramirez with Bonita. It was time to take her stitches out. The three-quarters dead dog that had snuggled up to me for the night and licked my face in gratitude (so I fondly thought) had been replaced by a raging beast, all teeth bared ready for action. As soon as she knew where she was the trouble started. Cristina was ready, somehow getting a muzzle on her, and she was bundled on to the table and tied down before I could even make an appearance. Pedro was impressed – not by our restraining techniques but by how strong the dog had become and how quickly she had recovered.

'She is a better guard dog now than ever,' he said. 'If any

ladrones are foolish enough to break into our property I will not need to feed her for a week.'

Just before lunch, the judge arrived to collect me in a brand new Renault. Most of the middle classes seemed to drive Renaults, proudly called 'The Colombian Car', which always amused me, as they were very French as far as I was concerned. First we went to his home to see the patient. For a superior judge Fernando lived modestly, although his house was large and in the Poblado district, of course, but it had no swimming-pool. It didn't need an expert to see that Poppy was doing well. After a quick check-up we headed on to the Club Campestre – the country club of Medellín.

I noticed that Fernando didn't have private bodyguards, which surprised me. 'No point,' he said, 'and a waste of money. If they want to kill me, they will, whatever. I'm careful, though.' He didn't elaborate further, concentrating instead on the short drive out to the club.

Within minutes I was in yet another world, passing through the guarded gates into a luxurious club for the privileged. In the car park, which was guarded, of course, a couple of boys – who had once been *gamines*, I imagined – had started up a nice little business valeting the members' cars. While we were away the car would be made spick and span.

We met up with Gloria's brothers-in-law, Jorge and Gustavo, by the huge outdoor swimming-pool. I hadn't seen them since Christmas so we spent the first few minutes catching up. A couple of waiters were bringing drinks to some beautiful young women lounging beside the pool. There was another bar at the other end, at which swimmers could order drinks without having to get out of the water. '*Hola*,' one of the women said to me as we passed.

I smiled back, wondering if I knew them, and nearly fell

in, much to the amusement of Gustavo who had witnessed the scene. 'When she realises you have no *plata* she'll lose interest,' he said, reading my mind. 'You're out of your league,' he added, with characteristic honesty. A well-dressed man of about thirty-five joined the two women as he spoke and I saw what he meant. The man had arrived in a Porsche just before us. Even though the girls hadn't seen the car, the cut of his clothes marked him out as being in the premier league that they were interested in.

We went over to the golf club-house to pick up some clubs for me and three caddies. It was nearly one o'clock and my stomach was already rumbling. I had thought we would eat before starting. 'Don't worry about food,' said Gustavo, again reading my mind. 'There are little bars and restaurants at every three or four holes. You won't stay hungry.'

This was the strangest round of golf I have ever played.

At the first two holes I didn't do too badly – or, at least, no worse than the others – taking half a dozen shots to get the ball down the hole. Then it was time to take a break. The third hole had a bar and a barbecue on site. We sat down and beers appeared, plus a huge *aguardiente* that I was supposed to down in one. I had found out in my short time in the country that watching the effect of *aguardiente* was a favourite sport of many Colombians. I downed it in one. 'Excellent quality,' I said. Jorge and Gustavo laughed. They knew me of old. We stocked up on kebab-type barbecued meat, called *chuzos*, which went well with the beer. Dessert would be at another hole.

When I stood up my knees were already feeling the effect of the drink and I felt peculiarly relaxed as I teed up for the next hole. Without trying too hard I swung the club at the ball and felt the satisfying crack as it struck right in the middle. 'Eh, *ave Maria*,' exclaimed the judge, in Spanish to Gustavo. 'That must be good *aguardiente*. You could wait years for a shot like that.'

I had lost sight of the ball as soon as I hit it, but apparently it had sailed high in the air and landed a couple of hundred yards away, plum in the middle of the fairway.

The effect of the *aguardiente* was short, though, as the next few shots were wayward and one dropped into a lake. By the sixth hole I was determined to do another blinding shot. It was a three-par hole and the green was clearly visible about two hundred yards away. I made an almighty swipe at the ball but just as my club came down to hit the ball, the frenzied barking of a dog sent it swerving off at about 45 degrees to the right. It disappeared into some bushes on the edge of the golf course. I swore at the dog, using words Diego had taught me while we were water-skiing.

For a moment there was a shocked pause and then the three Colombians were clutching their sides at the quaint Spanish I had just come out with. I left them to it, and went in search of the ball. Going through the bushes I crossed a track and saw the ball lying near a tin shack. A virtually naked boy of about ten beat me to it, picked it up and scuttled into the shack.

I had no alternative but to go and get it. As I approached it my first thought was that it was a dog kennel. I walked up to it and a woman came out with the boy holding her skirt. She held out her hand. 'Ten pesos.'

I fished in my pockets and found a ten-peso note, which I handed over. The boy threw the ball to me and they went into their home. I looked back and three more children were standing round their mother chattering excitedly and looking at the money.

I jogged back two hundred yards with the ball held aloft

to where the others were waiting for me, still highly amused by my choice turn of phrase. 'That is a very rude expression,' Fernando said, as we walked towards the green. 'If we had a queen in this country you wouldn't say anything like that in front of her.'

'It sounds nothing to me,' I said, which was the truth. It had no obvious meaning that I would have recognised. Swearing in another language somehow never sounds too bad. 'But I have had to pay for my sin. It cost me ten pesos to get the ball back.'

The others laughed. The going rate was one peso.

'There are families who live on that,' said Gustavo, and I nodded, adding that they seemed very poor.

'Further up the mountains there is no chance of any income. They have to live on what they can grow. Many of the children end up in Don Enrique's orphanage, and those are the lucky ones.'

We finished the round debating the fate of the poor. No one seemed to have the answer. 'Maybe Castro is right,' I suggested provocatively. Jorge and Gustavo raised their eyebrows. We could talk about such things privately but Fernando, after all, was a judge.

But they were wrong: Fernando was happy to join in the discussion. 'It wouldn't work here,' he said. 'The military is too strong. The guerrilla groups have been attempting revolution for decades. All that happens is a lot of people get killed. Nothing changes.' He paused to watch the ball trickle into the hole from thirty yards out.

'Time for another drink,' Jorge said, and the subject was closed.

Unlike the Spanish, Colombians often eat their evening meal early on and after the game was finished the whole family joined us at the club, with Don Enrique at the head, and once again I was treated to an excellent meal.

The contrast between the life of my friends and those in the *tugurios* couldn't have been more profound and my desire to carry on working in the clinic was fading rapidly. Teaching English to help people get better jobs seemed more worthwhile.

On the following Monday morning I had a case that showed me that although the job in Medellín wasn't as relevant as it had been at the Harmsworth it could still have its moments.

Dr Jaramillo, who worked at the local children's hospital, brought in his ten-year-old daughter's cat. This was unusual, since cats didn't figure highly on the average *paisa*'s must-get pet list. Popeye was a large ginger male that Eduardo had castrated a year or so back. He was the only vet prepared to do it and it had taken Cristina and the owners a few minutes to subdue it before it could be given an anaesthetic. For the most part it seemed that the local cats lived in proximity to humans but not often in their homes, making them more or less feral. Few people bothered much with the cats, except to give them food occasionally, and it was rare to see one in a vet's surgery. The effect of the castration had been, predictably, to turn Popeye into a home-loving cat that had taken to the little girl, and he spent most of his day near her. Isabella had called him Popeye, she told me, because of his large green eyes. She had come with her father and had clearly been crying. Popeye, it seemed, was the incarnation of loyalty and would follow the family car up the road until it was out of sight, and this had been his downfall.

When they had returned home from the family *finca* the previous night, they had found Popeye lying in the road. The doctor had brought him in and put him in a warm blanket, before taking him to his own hospital and X-raying him half-conscious. Now, at eight-thirty the following morning, Popeye was looking a bit more with it than he had the night before, but even without the X-ray I could see his hind leg was broken.

Dr Jaramillo was quite pleased with the quality of the X-ray, which was of the entire cat. It showed nothing obviously wrong except a clean break right in the middle of the thighbone. The two pieces were wide apart so something would have to be done to fix the break or Popeye would be crippled.

'We have surgeons who do this sort of work on children every day,' said Dr Jaramillo, 'but we wouldn't know where to start with this. I have rung round and nobody seems willing to do anything except amputate the leg. Can you fix it? You are our last hope.'

The fracture was a simple one of the type that I had seen virtually every day at the Harmsworth. I had brought some cat intravenous anaesthetic with me from England with just this kind of emergency in mind. I reckoned the surgery wouldn't take more than half an hour and I had plenty of anaesthetic.

There remained just one problem. I would need a Jacob's chuck, an intramedullary pin and a hacksaw blade. I spent a couple of minutes looking up 'hacksaw blade' in Spanish and drew pictures of the blade and the Jacob's chuck – there was no chance of finding *that* in a dictionary. Dr Jaramillo was unusual among educated Colombians in that he did not know much English. I had never been particularly good at art and Isabella looked at me pityingly. However Dr Jaramillo said he knew what I wanted and would get them from the hospital. 'I will be back within the hour,' he said, adding to his daughter, 'Don't worry, Mijita,

Popeye is going to be all right. We will operate later this morning.'

We? Well, I thought, as I gave the cat a sedative and waited for Dr Jaramillo's return, two pairs of hands were bound to be better than one.

Father and daughter duly arrived back on time with a hacksaw blade, a Jacob's chuck, which would hold the pin and allow me to drive it into the broken bone, and a selection of paediatric stainless-steel pins. Using the X-ray I selected the right pin for the job. We were ready to go.

'Do you mind if my daughter watches? She already wants to be a surgeon.'

'Not at all,' I replied. 'She can help Cristina. But if she feels faint, she's to tell you.'

A sleepy Popeye was soon under the anaesthetic and with the syringe strapped on to the leg with a large needle in the vein I reckoned I had enough anaesthetic to last an hour if need be. Dr Jaramillo and I scrubbed up and started.

'No gloves?' was his first remark.

'No,' I replied. 'Costs. But we have very little wound breakdown, you will see.'

I cut through one muscle layer and I was on to the broken bones. The pin fitted just right and within a few minutes the fragments were together. There was relatively little the doctor could do. After trimming the pin with the hacksaw blade it was time to sew up. I put a continuous stitch in the muscle layer and Dr Jaramillo stitched the skin together. He was highly amused and pleased. His daughter had solemnly watched the whole procedure, old beyond her years, with the occasional pertinent question. The beauty of the imported anaesthetic I had brought with me was the speed with which the patients came round: we had hardly finished a celebratory cup of coffee when

Popeye lifted his head, as if to say, 'What's all the fuss about?'

It had gone better than I could have hoped – only half an hour. The cat was ready to go home. I was amused as I saw them carrying him carefully out to the car. When I had first started at the Harmsworth three years before, I had wanted to keep all these cases in for a week, just in case anything went wrong. But the care Popeye would get at home would be better than even the best hospital nursing. And I didn't want another run-in with Pilar.

Since our row we had been studiously avoiding each other. But I had climbed down a bit and taken the padlock off the phone. Compared with London, phone calls were dirt cheap here and I had probably overreacted. But no way was I going to apologise. However, I had to step carefully because of Maria. While I taught Cristina English, Cristina was teaching Maria to read and write in Spanish and I knew she was making excellent progress. I didn't want anything to jeopardise that.

Maria's spoken Spanish, like that of most Colombians, even those with a poor education, was clear, and I benefited from chats with her, so it was a two-way thing. One day she asked me if I would be a godfather to her son. She was desperate to have him christened, but as a single parent she couldn't find a Colombian to do the job. I explained that I wasn't Catholic and that if I went back to England, which was likely, I might lose contact. The fact that I wasn't Catholic didn't seem to matter because there was a young, supposedly left-wing priest who didn't worry about such trivia, and if I was prepared to stand in, it would mean that the little boy, now eighteen months old, would have a name. I talked it over with Cristina and we agreed that both of us would be the little boy's godparents. He would be called David Ian, my names.

Before I knew it, the following Sunday I found myself in a small church in a poor suburb near to where Cristina lived. I understood little of the ceremony, which was part of the ordinary Sunday service. Medellín was a small world and it turned out that the young priest was a friend of Gloria's. Although I gathered he was very devout, he seemed to have time for the good life and didn't seem to mind that I wasn't Catholic. In fact, I got the distinct impression that in Colombia priests were not as celibate as their equivalents in Europe, and their priestly cover proved a good decoy when it came to affairs of the heart. They were also far more political than I had expected. This left-winger believed in contraception and happily forgave those who disobeyed the Church's ruling. He told me what to say – in Spanish, of course – and I had to lay my hand on the little boy's chest while I repeated the vows. There was applause when Ian David – they got the order of names wrong – was christened and he started to cry. I was moved to tears when I saw the joy on Maria's face.

Afterwards I felt deeply touched by the trouble Cristina had taken to make it a special day for Ian, as he was now called, and his mother. We had a celebratory lunch at her modest flat, prepared by her mother. There was a simple soup, some chicken and salad with a beer each and *aguardiente* afterwards to toast the child. The meal would have cost a couple of days' wages at least, but poor Colombians traditionally shared whatever they had. Their hospitality at all levels of society put us British in the shade, and I will never forget it.

Chapter 12

I had decided to walk into town. It was a lovely day, 22°C, and it really felt like spring. I found that I was eyeing up the girls more than I usually did. It was early February and coming up for St Valentine's Day. That gave me cause for thought: nearly six months and no girlfriend. No chance of a Valentine card for me, and no one to send one to. I thought briefly of Gloria and her new English boyfriend. A lawyer, apparently. A much better bet than a vet, I thought ruefully. But I felt no jealousy.

Ramón lived in the same district and we often met on the bus when we shared the same shift. Today as a bus came racing by, the driver hooting at a couple of gypsy girls, I saw a head swivel at the back, and realised it was Ramón, his eyes narrowed with incredulity. I just knew what he would say when he saw me next: 'You crazy gringo, walking into town.'

The gypsy girls obviously thought so too and immediately approached me. For ten pesos they would tell my fortune, they said. For a moment I was tempted. They were stunningly beautiful with flowing dark hair, instantly recognisable as *gitanas* by their striking, brightly coloured long dresses. Round their necks were strung an assortment of gaudy necklaces. If they were related in any way to European gypsies I never found out. However, just like gypsies all over the world they lived on the margins of society, surviving by their wits. They also had a reputation for being skilled pickpockets.

As the more beautiful of the two spoke to me I decided not to go down that route and elected to be the stupid non-Spanish-speaking gringo. 'No understand,' I said, in a heavily accented American voice.

'*Vea*,' the younger one said. See? I told you so. 'Let's not waste our time.' And they walked off contemptuously, their long dresses swaying in the wind.

I was soon on Calle 52, which would take me to the Avenida La Playa where the Institute of Modern English was situated. Walking right into the centre of town made me appreciate how much pollution there was: a pall of haze hung over the city. The crudely refined petrol, which most of the cars and buses ran on, belched out smelly fumes like urban dragons that made my eyes sting. But soon – in March I'd been told – the rainy season would begin and we would have torrential downpours every afternoon at four o'clock which would clear the atmosphere for a while and everything would smell fresh. The *paisas* called this season of regular rain 'winter', even though the temperature stayed at 22°C. As far as I was concerned every day felt like an English summer, without the fear that clouds would come over and the temperature would drop by ten degrees.

In town the *gamines* were out in force selling their contraband cigarettes. I wondered how legal cigarette vendors made any money. Legal tobacco was only sold in special kiosks.

I was amazed by the huge number of ways Colombians made a living. Some Indian women had set up a stall by the side of the road selling ponchos. Beside them were a couple of ragged children who were selling a couple of mango slices at a peso a time.

David Grant

I had no doubt that the mangoes had been stolen. Nothing was safe in this country, I had decided, unless it was chained to the ground, and then they'd probably steal the chain. And, of course, you couldn't escape the beggars. One with a toddler struck me: a tiny boy was walking in front of his father holding out his hand for money. The man had dark glasses and a white stick. The little boy had blond curly hair and looked angelic. I wondered if he really belonged to the man: blond children were not the norm, and the pesos were being handed over more liberally than usual and periodically he would trot back to his dad – or whoever it was – to hand over the proceeds. I decided I was becoming far too cynical in my old age.

I passed a shop that sold greetings cards and was surprised to see a huge placard taking up the whole of the window proclaiming that today was the Day of the Teacher. I ambled in. Teacher's Day might be today, but it seemed that every possible occupation had its day. There was a full list up beside the counter. Mother's Day, of course. I had even heard of Father's Day, but had always supposed that to be an American invention. But the Day of the Granny? And what about the Day of the Policeman? But I suppose it was logical. If you were a card manufacturer why restrict yourself to Christmas and birthdays? It was heartening to see so many people buying cards for teachers.

Five minutes later I arrived at the Institute to find, to my amazement, that I was the recipient of about fifteen. I had never had so many cards, even on my birthday. All, of course, were from girls. Who needed Valentine's Day? This was far better; they were signed and covered with kisses.

At the start of my last class of the day, a pretty elfin-faced girl announced that they were throwing an impromptu party for me, and we all trooped out towards the Pasaje Junin.

But then one by one they spotted friends and said, 'Sorry, perhaps next week.' We were soon down to four: me, Ramón and two girls. The elfin-faced one was called Marta and her friend Consuelo. As we snaked our way down Pasaje Junin, Ramón confided in me that Marta was *tragada* with me. He made an imaginary slit of the throat as he said the word.

I thought hard. Tragedy? Dead?

'She's crazy about you, man,' he said, in his Al Capone English. 'And I'm in with Consuelo.'

'Please speak in Spanish,' Marta said, slipping her hand into mine.

This was very forward, at least to an Englishman. I glanced at Ramón, but he was deep in conversation with Consuelo.

Marta was no more than twenty, but like most Colombian young women she was immaculately dressed and made up – there was nothing about either girl that said student, in the English sense of jeans and unwashed hair.

They were very alike – to the point where they might have been sisters – and very pretty.

We went into one of the restaurants in Pasaje Junin and Ramón ordered two beers. The girls had Coca-Cola. As soon as the beers arrived Marta poured mine for me and Consuelo did the same for Ramón.

'Colombian girls, they know how to look after men,' he confided in English, his eyes lighting up at future prospects. But he was in for a disappointment. It was a set-up. Consuelo, it turned out, had only come along for the ride. She already had a boyfriend. In order to make her position clear she began talking about this man, who was an undertaker.

'Do you have a boyfriend?' I asked Marta casually.

'I am looking for one,' she replied, giving me a meaning-ful smile. We had another round of beers and Coca-Colas, then it was time to head home. Neither of the two girls came originally from Medellín and both were staying with relatives. They had to be home by nine unless permission had been obtained; normally a chaperone would have come too. After seeing the girls to their bus, Ramón said he wanted to play some pool and knew a pool hall not far away where the beer was cheap.

'So Consuelo has an undertaker boyfriend, does she?' I said, as we walked along. 'You'd better keep your hands off or you'll end up as one of her boyfriend's clients.' There was an element of truth in this. The word was that the *serenata* groups, with their love songs, were being replaced by *sicarios* – hired guns. They could be found without difficulty, particularly at night, and instead of going round to sing six songs outside your girlfriend's window, they would simply eliminate anyone you didn't like. For example, a rival. And the going rate was only fifty dollars – quite a lot for a Colombian but by no means outlandish.

'And now I remember what I wanted to say to you.' Ramón had stopped in his tracks and turned to me, looking more like a Cherokee Indian than usual. 'Didn't I see you walking to town today? Are you crazy? In this town nobody walks. Period.' He went on to detail the various scams that might befall the unwary gringo. 'And don't kid yourself. You may think you look like one of us with your dark hair and tan, but don't forget your blue eyes. You're a gringo. Nobody in Colombia has blue eyes. Do yourself a favour. At least buy yourself a pair of shades. And as for the shoes, man . . .' His gaze shifted to my feet – my English brogues were still in reasonable condition after regular attention from the shoe-blacks. 'Those are like a neon sign on your forehead. You stand no chance. Get some like these.'

He lifted up a foot clad in soft light brown suede with what looked like a rope sole. A sad, overweight woman brought us our beers as we started a game of pool. I glanced at her, wondering how much she got paid for working in this dive. She was the only woman in the place. The toilet arrangements were pretty primitive and in full view of her. She had an incipient moustache from which beads of sweat occasionally erupted. Her skirt was hitched ludicrously up near her midriff and her high heels made it difficult for her to walk. Even with these she only came up to my shoulder. She never seemed to smile.

Ramón spotted me looking at her. 'Hey, gringo, you want to get to know her a bit better?' His eyes rolled lasciviously. 'Before you do, you need to pay that guy over there a fine.' He gestured with his eyes at a thin, mealy-mouthed man with a pencil moustache behind the bar. At that point the man looked up at me and nodded quizzically towards the woman. I couldn't believe I was only a nod away from a fate worse than death.

I shook my head as casually as I could muster and made a gesture indicating that I wanted two more beers. He shrugged his shoulders and ordered the waitress to bring them over. 'I think I can organise my own love-life, thank you, Ramón,' I said. At first I thought he had been joking but now I realised he was half serious. 'You said yourself that Marta was mad about me.' It was hard not to allow a certain smugness to creep into my voice.

Ramón roared with laughter. 'This is Colombia, David. You won't be seeing any action with her until she has a ring on her finger.' He settled down to potting the balls with the skill acquired during his misspent youth in New York.

I thought about it for a minute. Ramón was always exaggerating. I knew things were different in Colombia, but not that different, surely. The signs had all been there.

Towards midnight I realised I hadn't eaten. At the end of the road there was a Kentucky Fried Chicken-type place called Kokorico that would do nicely. As we were leaving I was astonished to see the little blond boy that I had seen begging in the streets earlier in the day walk into the bar with his father.

When I had seen the pair earlier, the question in my mind had been whether the man was actually his father. It hadn't occurred to me that the con they were running was even more cynical: the man wasn't even blind. Here, in the safety of a neighbourhood pool hall, he had abandoned his dark glasses and white stick and could obviously see. The little boy was made to sit at the table near the pool table and a bottle of *aguardiente* appeared. I was furious but Ramón stopped me going over and demanding to know why the three-year-old was still out at nearly midnight while his father was downing the profits. 'Keep cool man,' he warned. The man would no doubt have a knife. He would need it to fend off other villains.

Sickened, I left – suddenly not hungry after all. I decided to walk home. Ramón tried to dissuade me but I reckoned I would be safe enough on the main road back to the clinic, which was only fifty yards off this road. 'OK, but don't walk behind parked cars and don't stop to talk if anyone says anything,' was Ramón's last piece of advice as we parted company.

In the event the walk passed off uneventfully. There was hardly anyone about and there was a chill in the air. Being at five thousand feet had its advantages. I crept into the house and all was quiet. Maybe the whole security thing was exaggerated.

It was a topic I brought up with Dan the next afternoon at the language school. I had gone in early, having had a dull morning in the clinic with just a couple of vaccinations to do. The vaccination market had plummeted when the word got round that I wouldn't crop ears or dock tails. The clients wanted unnecessary surgery on virtually every dog, not just the breeds that were traditionally done – like Dobermans. I refused to do it, and Cristina had given up trying to change my mind. Enough money was coming in from the surgical cases. Another surgeon's dog was booked in to see me tomorrow.

In the meantime I felt in need of some English conversation – I could only take Ramón in small doses – and Dan was a good listener. Strangely for someone who was so religious, Dan tended to keep off the subject of God.

'Well, I've been here eighteen months,' he said, when I asked if he'd experienced any violence, 'and I've never had a problem. You just have to watch your back. Believe me, it's no worse than Houston.' And in build Dan was no pro footballer. He was no taller than many Colombians, though years of Texan living had left him solid rather than reedy. Nobody he knew had been ripped off, he went on, and mostly it was quiet where he lived in the centre. 'When you get a Friday-afternoon riot you need to be careful,' he went on. 'Then all the crooks in town take advantage of the chaos and you might have trouble. We haven't had one of those in a while, though.'

Friday-afternoon riot?

'In fact,' Dan continued, 'we should be due for one. You can kind of feel it in your nostrils. There's tension in the air. I noticed it on the way here this morning, as a matter of

169

fact. What's today? Tuesday. Give it a couple of days and we'll see.'

He went back to reading the Bible. He always seemed to have three or four on him – in Spanish, of course – and he was set on reading it all, improving his Spanish at the same time.

One of the reasons Dan rarely talked about religion was that Tom, the other American teacher, was always primed to start a discussion that might easily turn into an argument. Unusually for an American – in my experience – Tom was a card-carrying atheist and was always trying to challenge Dan's faith. They were a strange pair: Dan small and intense, introverted, Tom rangy, with fiery red hair and a droopy moustache to match. Their views on the world were as different as their appearance.

There was nothing that Tom wouldn't argue about, just for the sake of it more often than not. He was always being contrary, as my grandmother used to say. For a start, except when he was teaching, he always spoke Spanish, even with me. He had immersed himself completely in the local culture and spoke like an Antioquian. He talked so fast that when he was arguing with Ramón – which he often did – Dan and I couldn't follow. And once I'd lost the thread of the argument I'd spend the rest of my break looking out from my ringside seat on the veranda at the world go by below.

I can't say I enjoyed my four-hour stints at the college, but even so it didn't seem like work and time always went quickly. Having a captive audience of pretty women helped. The week following our trip to Pasaje Junin, Marta told me that her sister Helena was coming, and would I like to join them for a drink. Helena was slightly older than Marta and looked less like her sister than Consuelo did. I was left in no doubt that I was being appraised. Helena had brought her fiancé, Paco, with her. He spoke no English but demonstrated the usual Colombian hospitality and insisted on buying the drinks. He said he was thinking of learning English too, but that he was waiting to see how Marta got on. I was the first Englishman any of them had met.

This time we went to a restaurant-cum-club that seemed to be a regular haunt. We snacked on *empanadas* and the inevitable *aguardiente* and danced. This time there was no nine o'clock curfew: chaperoned by her sister and Paco, Marta could stay out late and it was midnight by the time we got back to the modest terraced house where both girls lived with their relations.

A peck on the cheek and Marta went in. Five minutes later Helena and Paco dropped me off outside the clinic and waited until I was safely inside. A smile, a flash of the lights, and they roared off. I had passed the test, it seemed, and could be considered a prospective *novio*.

I crept up the stairs and collapsed in a heap on the bed, too tired to wonder or care if a *novio* was what I wanted to be right now. It didn't help that the translation of *novio* was fiancé. Fiancé? I had barely kissed her.

I slept late and was awakened by Maria. Cristina was already downstairs and the first patient had arrived.

I showered and dressed in record time, but didn't have time to shave. Not that it mattered: compared to most Colombians I was very clean-shaven.

It was a surgeon from the same hospital as the owner of Popeye the cat. Word was obviously out, I decided.

I was swiftly disabused of this idea. He was only coming to me, he said, because two other vets had told him that a growth on his dog's leg was inoperable and he should be put down. A third had said the leg would have to come off and a fourth agreed to operate but didn't offer much hope.

It was at this point that he'd heard about *el inglés* from his colleague. I was the last resort.

In England if I had seen an animal already under another vet's care without his permission I could have been struck off the vets' register. Here, they didn't seem to take much notice of professional ethics and I had long since given up asking Cristina to ring the other vets concerned.

Dr Ricardo Marulanda seemed young to be a surgeon – he looked about twenty-five. His Spanish was refined and he spoke slowly. For the first time I found that I was understanding every word he said, even with the *paisa* accent. He had studied medicine in Medellín, which I already knew had several excellent hospitals. Such was the city's fame that patients were sometimes seen from other Latin-American countries.

My patient was a ten-year-old boxer with the unlikely name of Horatio. He had been a graduation present to the newly qualified Dr Marulanda from his family. I did a few sums. The doctor couldn't possibly be twenty-five, more like thirty-five. In the end I asked him and, yes, I was right. When I looked taken aback he explained that he was a fitness fanatic and went to the gym three times a week. The dog had stayed with Ricardo when he got married and now, with three young children on the scene, was very much part of the family, which was why he wanted to save him if there was the remotest chance.

At first sight the growth looked pretty nasty. It was large and between the toes on the right front leg, an angry dark colour with patches of ulceration. Horatio wouldn't let me look at it closely.

'When was he last fed?' I asked.

'I starved him just in case you wanted to operate,' was

the reply. I looked at my watch – it was just after eleven. It shouldn't take more than an hour. 'Can I help?'

'Of course,' I replied, although I felt momentary panic. I explained that the anaesthetic was intravenous only, which he accepted as it was common practice in rural areas. Of course, he would have operated in the countryside under similar conditions. Because Horatio was a boxer I didn't give him a pre-med injection. At home we used Valium to sedate boxers because the routine drug for most dogs was too strong for them. We relied on sitting with the dog after the operation and trying to keep it calm.

Five minutes later Horatio was asleep on Eduardo's stainless-steel operating table. We scrubbed up and took a look at the tumour. Ricardo pulled it up as far as it would go and I was pleasantly surprised to find that it had a stalk. If, as Ricardo suggested, we did an elliptical incision, we should be able to get it all out and still have enough skin to play with in the stitching-up process.

Ricardo couldn't resist doing the initial surgery with my help. Cristina came up with the excellent idea of using the hand cautery set that Eduardo used in ear-cropping to seal off the bleeding vessels. Within fifteen minutes the growth had been removed. Ricardo put in four stitches and Horatio came round almost immediately. Luck was on our side because his recovery was smooth, rather than the howling and thrashing about that sometimes happens with an unsedated dog.

At a quarter to twelve Horatio was sitting up, ready to be transported home. Ricardo had brought with him some formalin pots just in case he was successful in persuading me to operate. He put a couple of pieces of the tumour in them to have them analysed by the hospital pathology department.

I was pleased: it couldn't have gone better and as good

a job had been done as might be expected in the best of hospitals. We would now have to wait for the pathologist's verdict but I had a feeling that we were home and dry.

With the clinic two thousand pesos richer, I decided to take the afternoon off and go the Colombo-Americano library in town and while away a few hours reading. There were no books in English in Eduardo's house, apart from his textbooks, and I had in mind something that would take me out of myself. I wasn't quite up to reading books in Spanish. Relatively speaking, they seemed a lot more expensive in Colombia than they were in England. A sudden wave of nostalgia came over me: two important ingredients of my previous life in England were missing here – music and reading. I sighed and jumped on the bus to town.

Chapter 13

In England, whether in Kent or in London, the first thing I did every morning was open the curtains and look at what sort of day it was. In Kent it had affected everything: when the rain was hammering down, my heart would sink at the thought of ploughing across fields and getting drenched having to deal with a cow that had collapsed perhaps miles from the farmhouse; if the sun was shining my spirits rose at the thought of a day spent cruising around the Kent countryside, watching lambs frolicking on the spring grass, or even having a sandwich and a shandy outside a pub.

I still looked out of the window every morning, but nothing ever changed: it was always a fine day. The next morning was the same as every other. Cristina was already busy when I joined her downstairs. Sometimes I wondered what she did – compared with the Harmsworth, updating records was more of a pastime than a job.

A Yorkie came in with an upset stomach – what Eduardo would have called an overloaded liver. It didn't really matter what treatment it was given, it would get better eventually – it was the equivalent of a human having a touch of indigestion. I told Cristina as much – but she looked at me as if I was a silly little boy who didn't understand that unless you tie your shoelaces you will fall over. I knew I was on a hiding to nothing. No drugs meant no fee. I gave in and Cristina typed up the normal list of medicines that Eduardo served up on these occasions.

While she was clacking away the telephone rang and I answered it. It was an extremely worried-sounding Janina. Bosun was not eating properly. He had refused his toast and caviar that morning.

This was more like it. The caviar might have to be tested, I decided. The last time I had been offered it I had only managed a couple of bites, but I had begun to understand its appeal. I couldn't believe that I had descended to the level of eating a dog's reject food but my staple diet of beans and beans had palled.

Curiously, although I ate huge portions, I had lost weight and was now down to around 75 kilos. Marta had weighed me a few days before in a newly installed machine outside a pharmacy in the town centre. She was concerned that I was too thin and had resolved to sort this out with frequent snacks of cheese and guava jelly whenever I went to her house, which was becoming a frequent occurrence. I had taken to it.

As I left the office, Cristina warned me to take care. Her mother had heard talk of trouble on the streets. 'Take your passport,' she said, 'just to be sure.'

I remembered what Dan had said about there being the smell of riots in the air. I hadn't detected it but I had been long enough in Colombia to listen to what people were saying.

I went upstairs to change. I always tried to make myself reasonably smart for my trips to the Schwarzkopfs. The better I looked, I reasoned, the more they were likely to pay me. Also Ramón, Marta and myself were going to eat at somewhere a bit more special than our usual haunts after classes. I grabbed a small briefcase I had brought from England and popped my passport into it, just in case. I didn't want the DAS heavies locking me up for lack of ID.

¡Viva El Vet!

Cristina had ordered a taxi for me, knowing that Janina would pay at the other end.

'Don't hesitate to phone me if anything comes in that can't wait until tomorrow,' I said. This was my standard parting shot, though Cristina had never taken me up on it. But there was always a first time. Even though the Institute was paying me much more than the clinic, a sick animal would always take priority.

'Take care, Dr David,' Cristina replied, demonstrating her concern by flicking her wrist at the thought of what might happen in the centre of town as the day wore on.

I laughed and gave her a cheery English wave. She worried too much, I decided. And her mother worried too much. But as the taxi sped along I remembered again, with a sense of unease, what Dan had said about the city being due for a riot. Yet it was hard to believe: it was about eleven o'clock and seemed hotter than usual; as for atmosphere, the city seemed about as tense as a towel. As for worrying, it seemed to be a national characteristic, at least as far as the women in this city were concerned.

I arrived on time. As usual, Bosun was delighted to see me, bouncing about and barking. He seemed in the peak of condition.

'You look rather warm, David. Let me take your jacket,' Janina said. As she took it she seemed to find it necessary to brush up against me. It was then I noticed that instead of the usual smart suit or fitted trousers she favoured, she was wearing a flowing white dress, which when she stood in front of the window – and she spent a lot of time standing in front of the window – didn't leave much to the imagination. The word négligée floated into my mind, although I had no idea what one looked like. As I looked into Bosun's mouth she leaned right over me and the smell of what must have

177

been incredibly expensive perfume nearly suffocated me. Now I could see clearly that she wasn't wearing anything underneath her dress.

'He wouldn't eat his caviar,' she said, in a voice that seemed lower than usual.

'Let me have a try,' I said, trying to sound casual, in a voice that seemed a good deal higher than usual.

A minute later, she returned with a silver tray, a bowl – also silver with a silver spoon – and a plate of thin biscuits.

'I'm sorry,' I said. 'I didn't mean you to go to any trouble.'

'That's all right,' she purred. 'I enjoy doing little things when I'm on my own.'

'So Ernst's not here, then?'

'No. And I've given the maid the afternoon off, so I'm quite alone . . . We're quite alone.' A tinkly laugh filled the room.

The situation was delicate, I decided, but not delicate enough to prevent me sampling the most luxurious food in the world. I might never get another chance. And, anyway, I had to do something to defuse the situation.

'Mind if I try some?' I said. 'Psychology,' I added, in explanation. 'Maybe he'll want some himself if he sees me eating.'

I proceeded to help myself, spreading the tiny black globes on to the biscuits. I placed myself directly in Bosun's line of vision. Now I had two pairs of eyes staring at me. Well, I might as well eat. The texture was interesting, I decided, though whether pleasant or not I couldn't make up my mind. Similarly the taste. Fishy, but not that fishy. Bosun had moved and was now sitting immediately in front of me watching my every move. I had another. He licked his lips.

Then I prepared a third. I let him wait until I had a good spoonful of it on the biscuit then casually threw it to him.

A flying leap worthy of Nureyev – and he swallowed it in one graceful movement.

'Cured,' I pronounced.

'Thank you, thank you, my hero.' Even more quickly than Bosun snapping the caviar, Janina's face loomed above mine and then she kissed me full on the lips. 'Ernst won't be back till this evening,' she added, taking my arm and moving me towards the door. 'And he's terribly understanding.'

The sound of the garage-door mechanism saved me. Ernst.

'My God – I don't believe it,' she muttered under her breath, and hurried upstairs.

When Ernst came into the room, I was feeding the dog bits of biscuit and caviar and he was salivating all over the carpet. Ernst looked puzzled. 'Someding wrong vid de dog?'

Before I had a chance to answer Janina appeared, dressed in a red dress down to her ankles. 'He refused his breakfast, darling, and you know how I worry so. Dr Grant came straight away.'

Ernst gave me a what's-going-on-here look. The word Gestapo sprang to mind, and I decided to make tracks.

'Sometimes when dogs have a stomach upset they refuse things they know they shouldn't have,' I said.

'Hah. Like caviar,' retorted Ernst triumphantly.

Janina gave me fifteen dollars, which would include the taxi back. I did not meet her eye but busied myself with putting on my jacket. I made my farewells and left them to it, sensing a row in the offing.

I had ten pesos in my pocket and decided to catch a bus into town and change the dollars later. I had plenty of adrenaline to work off and, anyway, fifteen dollars would feed me for a week. I scuttled down the drive as if my life depended on it.

It was getting even hotter and I was beginning to regret both the jacket and tie. I was just considering trying to find a taxi when a rickety old bus came into view, comparatively empty. I waved and the driver stopped. They were only too happy to take as many passengers as possible and didn't adhere to bus stops. I felt uneasy as soon as I got on and paid my peso fare. This was surely the oldest bus in the fleet.

There were no doors or glass in the windows. The gear lever went straight into the gearbox, whose inner workings were clearly visible – must make maintenance simple, I thought. There was a stench of burning oil so I elected to sit on the back seat by the open door. This was second nature now – Ramón's tip: it guaranteed a quick exit if necessary.

The bus rumbled on towards the centre, picking up the odd passenger. Nobody seemed to want to get off. Gradually it filled up and I began to sense that I might have made a mistake. The reason the bus had been empty was simply that the Schwarzkopf ranch was way out of town. Next, I was distinctly overdressed and, yes, I had my best gringo shoes on and no sunglasses. As for the briefcase, what did I think I was doing? I might as well have been wearing a diamond-encrusted Rolex.

Subconsciously I hugged it close to my body and put the other hand in my pocket containing the precious fifteen dollars. People would kill for less.

We were still on the outskirts of town when I was aware of two hard-looking men staring at me from half-way down the bus.

'*Pilas con el gringo*,' one of them said. Let's get him. They clearly did not expect me to understand – I mean, only an idiot foreigner with no knowledge of Spanish would get on to a bus like this.

A few of the other passengers turned to look at me, fear transforming their usually happy faces. The men were slowly moving towards me, pushing their way through the centre aisle, packed with people. I saw one of them reach into his pocket for something – in all probability a knife. What should I do? I could jump, but the bus was moving at the usual breakneck speed. And break neck is what would happen. So, what next? Fight? Shout and scream? Neither would help. The other passengers would do nothing. I would be dead if I tried to resist.

With a sense of rising panic I tried to work out how the attack would come. As they got nearer there was a sudden sharp braking with much hooting and swearing. We had narrowly missed colliding with another bus. As a result we slowed to about fifteen miles per hour. The only reason for not jumping – breaking my neck – had disappeared. I had a fraction of a second to decide what to do.

I jumped out of the back entrance through the non-existent door and hit the ground running. It was a fairly busy road and I took off like a rugby three-quarter with the briefcase under my arm.

I heard a shout behind me, glanced back and saw the two men chasing me. They had jumped too. This wasn't an area with friendly (to me) watchmen on guard at the entrance to sweeping drives whom I could persuade to help me. I was in Guayaquil, reputed to be one of the toughest areas of town – I recognised the streets from previous trips through it with the Ruiz'. I could hear Gustavo's voice in my head: 'Don't even think of going there. You would never get out.'

I decided to turn right along a quieter street where I could really sprint. I couldn't believe it. I had always reckoned

I'd be a match for anyone, but the two villains seemed to be gaining on me. When I turned into the side-street I took off.

At the end, after about four hundred yards, I came to another main road. I allowed myself a quick look behind. No one. I had lost them. With a sigh of relief I took my bearings. I was on Calle 50. I knew that this would take me up to the Berrio Park.

I walked up the road as nonchalantly as possible, mopping the sweat from my face with a tissue. Within five minutes I was in the park. I could get another bus from here to the Institute.

I was surprised to see a large crowd of young people gathered outside the government building, so needing to rest and get my breath back I stopped to see what it was all about.

'Teachers' wages,' a friendly-looking student told me. 'They are exploited by the *corbatas*.' This was a negative term, meaning 'ties', referring to white-collar workers who wear them – people we would probably call suits, these days.

There was a crackling tension in the air and I fingered my own tie nervously. I decided to remove it. I undid the knot with one hand, holding tight to my briefcase with the other.

I was just walking away when, without warning, the students pushed like football fans towards the steps of the building and I was carried along with them. The reason was soon apparent. A comical figure had appeared at the front steps of the building – comical because he was wearing theatrical-looking army uniform complete with white boots and puffed-up chest. He resembled something out of a Gilbert and Sullivan opera. He stood immobile. I couldn't help feeling that he made the perfect target – even Eduardo could have scored a bullseye. His contempt for the crowd was equally matched by their contempt for him. Whistles and catcalls were followed by chanting – they were telling him he was an example of the type of person who was 'damaging the nation'.

A street urchin standing about a yard in front of me hurled a stone in his direction – it landed harmlessly at his feet. But that had been what this monstrous character was waiting for. He reached into his jacket and I flinched. I was convinced he was getting out a gun. But it was a mobile radio, what we called in those days a walkie-talkie. He pulled out the aerial and immediately started barking orders into it. Within seconds, fifty or more troops poured out of the door behind him and emerged from the side of the building, running towards us, doing a kind of goose-step. I was fascinated, mesmerised and appalled. I didn't move, I just watched: to me the goose-stepping appeared more ridiculous than menacing. But the crowd weren't as docile, and this display of military might provoked a rain of stones and bricks that descended on the troops like black hailstones.

Pandemonium ensued and the goose-stepping was replaced by an outright chase. The students ran in all directions. I couldn't believe it – the second time in one day that I had to get the hell out of it. Perhaps because I was tired I decided to go the other way and play the part of the innocent bystander caught up in something that was none of his doing. A businessman.

As nonchalantly as I could I walked, with the briefcase prominent, towards the corner of the park. The restaurants and bars I passed were being hastily boarded up, ready for the storm. Soldiers rushed past me under the direction of several officers. It was as if I was invisible. Walkie-talkies were everywhere. Those people who were considered ring-leaders were being rounded up and rifle butts were used to knock them down. Half a dozen students were caught and as each one collapsed he received a kicking for good measure and one soldier was detailed to stand guard. It wasn't only male students who suffered: I saw one older woman, screaming what was obviously her son's name, get a blow in the stomach for her trouble.

Meanwhile, other soldiers stood guard over a pile of rubble, which might have been used as student ammu-nition. I carried on walking away, heading for the Institute and safety.

Once I was on the Avenida La Playa, which was only four hundred yards from the Institute, I thought I would be safe. But things suddenly turned nasty. Gangs of youths were stopping cars, making the drivers get out, then turning the cars over and torching them. There must have been half a dozen burning at the side of that one road. In places a pitched battle raged with students throwing Molotov cocktails – bottles filled with petrol, which smashed and burst into flames – through office and bank windows. There was an acrid stench of smoke everywhere. The whistles and catcalls had ceased. Now the sound was of sirens and horns, shouts of terror.

I sprinted the last few hundred yards in blind panic. I could see Tom sitting on the balcony viewing the proceedings with excitement – he might have been watching extra time at a football match. He was so involved he didn't hear me shouting below: 'For God's sake, let me in.' Finally one of his tame *gamines* attracted his attention and he vanished, then reappeared at the glass door, which he opened, grabbed me and closed it again, sliding the bolt across the bottom with a thud.

¡Viva El Vet!

The scene upstairs resembled a war zone with fifty or so students and half a dozen teachers huddled in the main coffee bar area. All lessons had been suspended. I looked for Marta, but she had been forewarned and had gone straight home. In a corner Dan was being consoled by Jairo. He was wrapped up in a poncho, his bare, pale legs sticking out below it.

'What's up?' I asked.

'I've been mugged,' he replied. I immediately thought of our previous conversation, about how safe the city was, and was about to make a remark, then thought better of it. It was no time for jokes. Apparently two men had come up to him on the Avenida La Playa and got him in a bear hug. They were pretending to be delighted to see him after a long time. He passed out and when he came to he was lying in a shop doorway, with only his shirt and underpants. The thieves had stolen his clothes, money, glasses, even his Bibles. This was what had upset him the most. One of the students had spotted him and a couple had got him up to the Institute where he was now trying to come to terms with it all.

He was shivering in shock and I could see that his mouth was moving in prayer.

'Troops!' Tom shouted out. 'OK. Time to get our heads down, guys.' As he spoke there was a stutter of small-arms fire. From inside the building I could just see that the crowd was being pushed up the avenue towards us and smashing what they could – windows, cars, doors – on the way.

Suddenly a large brick crashed through the window near to where I was standing, making a dent in the wall, and a trickle of dark plaster ran down the white wall.

Almost immediately someone shouted, 'Gas!'

For a moment I wasn't sure if this was true, then I was choking, tears streaming down my face. I hadn't been crying

before but suddenly the tears turned into genuine ones and I
was fighting for my breath.

I had never thought tear gas sounded very drastic, but
it was. It was like being punched in the nose. Not only
unpleasant but very painful. I copied the others, taking off
my shirt and using it to cover my eyes and nose. It was
chaos, with people coughing and shouting to each other.
Those who'd been through it before kept their heads close
to the ground. I wondered how long the effects would last.

Suddenly Ramón grabbed me. 'We gotta get the hell out
of here,' he hissed. 'That is, if you don't want to spend the
night in this dump.'

'Don't be insane,' I said. 'We'll be killed if we go out
in that.'

Ramón laughed. 'These guys, they hate anything American.'

'But it's called the Institute of Modern English,' I protested.

'Americans talk English. You're all gringos. Anything
English or American is a legitimate target.'

The idea of leaving the solid safety of the Institute for the
mayhem of the streets did not immediately appeal.

'Do you trust me, gringo? Have I ever let you down?'

This wasn't the moment for a loyalty test.

'Listen. I have this uncle. He's a priest, lives not far.
Priests are like Switzerland in this place. You know, safe.
Nobody touches them, especially not the cops or the little
soldier boys.'

I nodded in agreement.

'OK. First take your watch off and leave the briefcase
here. And dump the jacket.'

We made our way downstairs and slipped out of a side
door. It was strangely quiet. The action seemed to have
moved a few streets away. A dozen cars were still burning.

¡Viva El Vet!

The smell was something I shall never forget: tear gas, petrol, burning rubber.

'Walk, don't run unless you have to,' Ramón said. I followed him. We made our way to Pasaje Junin, then through a catacomb of side-streets until Ramón put up his hand, stopped and knocked at a small door.

It was opened in seconds by a small middle-aged priest – Ramón had phoned him before we left to say we were on our way. We went through and the door clanged shut behind us. A rapid-fire unintelligible conversation followed. Ramón didn't want a bolthole, he wanted out. After more rapid-fire *paisa*, he beckoned me to follow and the priest opened a door that led into an internal garage. We were told to get into the back of the car. We crouched in the footwells and put our heads on the back seat. The priest covered us with a foul-smelling blanket.

I heard the garage doors being opened, the priest got in, started up the engine, then slowly edged the car out.

He drove to the nearest *avenida*, then slowly made his way through the centre to the other side of town. I couldn't see what was going on but could hear the occasional smash and whoosh as a Molotov cocktail was launched. Again the smell of tear gas filtered through the car windows and my eyes were smarting – but the priest was made of sterner stuff and drove on relentlessly, if slowly.

'They won't stop him when they see his dog collar,' Ramón whispered. I looked at him: the usual grin, and inevitable cigarette hanging out of the side of his mouth. I couldn't believe it – the blanket might catch fire. I tried to mime this – as I saw it, quite reasonable – fear, but Ramón just grinned.

After ten nervous minutes we were told the coast was clear.

David Grant

I looked uneasily out of the window, but everything here seemed normal. Not a soldier or a burning car in sight.

'How far out of town are we?' I asked Ramón. I didn't recognise the area.

'About five K,' he said. 'Hungry?' he asked, after his uncle had dropped us outside a restaurant. When I didn't answer, he continued, 'Well, gringo, that'll make something interesting to write on your postcards home.'

I wasn't hungry, whether through fear or the effect of the tear gas I didn't know.

I accepted a beer. It was a balmy evening and groups of diners were sitting outside without a care in the world. A beer had never tasted so good. And yes, I decided, perhaps I could manage something to eat. Though I still had no money – except the fifteen dollars from Janina. Ramón said not to worry. I could pay him back another time.

We were only three miles from the worst violence I had ever seen and we might as well have been in a different country, except that I could still hear the whine of sirens, muffled explosions and plumes of smoke lazily snaking upwards.

While we were waiting for our food a group of musicians approached us and asked if we wanted a song. Gesturing towards the mayhem that I knew was the city centre, I asked for '*Pueblito Viejo*'.

They laughed, as did some of the other diners, and played it as well as I had ever heard it. Ramón bought me another beer. But I owed him more than a couple of beers: he had saved me from an unpleasant night and even more danger. We watched and wondered if there would be an Institute to teach in tomorrow.

Chapter 14

The next day I couldn't believe how calm everything was. In fact, if you had slept through the whole thing and missed a day, you wouldn't have known anything was different.

In the centre of the city the odd broken window was proof that the whole thing hadn't been a figment of my imagination, but that was it. Everything was quiet, people were walking about as usual, the buses hurtling through the traffic. It was as though there had been a massive blow-out and that had been enough to settle things down for a while – rather like a marital row.

There was no tension on the streets. A few days later I read an account of the riot in the newspapers: apparently left-wing extremists had hijacked a peaceful demonstration and turned it into an anti-government riot; anti-social delinquents had jumped on the bandwagon, forcing the hand of the security forces. But it had had tragic consequences: two students had been shot dead, and countless 'criminal' elements had been detained awaiting trial. No further information was forthcoming and this did not change. After a week or so it was as though the riot had never happened.

If I had learned anything it was to make myself scarce whenever the word was out that a demonstration was about to happen. Marta was adamant on that point, and she made it clear that I was a fool to have ventured into town when all the indications were that there was going to be major trouble. Ramón, meanwhile, had organised a trip to a shanty town on the hillsides overlooking the town. It was time, he said, that I had a little political education. It turned out that his uncle the priest was of left-wing tendencies and therefore spent a lot of his time ministering to the poor. I wasn't surprised.

A week or so later the three of us set out to visit a shanty town not far from the Poblado district. Ramón had briefed me before we set out.

'We'll probably be OK, but dress down. Scuff your shoes. The trousers are OK.'

I had just bought them: they were dark red. I had to laugh. It was unthinkable to wear red trousers in England, but here it wasn't just normal, it was safe. My shirt was yellow with blue triangles. I had to find myself a pair of cheap sunglasses – my blue eyes still caused people to stare – leave my watch at home, but be sure to take fifty pesos in cash in case we were mugged. If we had any less, the muggers might get angry, and then who knew what might happen?

The three of us drove to El Poblado where the priest left his car, then started walking up the mountain. As we walked, I talked to Joachim, Ramón's uncle, and told him how much I appreciated his help during the riot. He was pleasant but had other things on his mind: he wasn't in the mood for an English-style chat.

Soon the roads began to appear neglected and finally petered out to become dirt tracks. As we climbed higher the view of Medellín was increasingly beautiful. At the same time the houses were rougher and rougher, until finally we were in a true shanty town. If we hadn't been with Joachim, I knew that it might have been nasty, but he was obviously well known, and as we walked up the dusty road people called out to him – sometimes just a greeting, sometimes because they wanted to talk to him. From time to time we would stop while he heard some tale of woe. He listened attentively, then said something that seemed to cheer the sufferer. I hardly understood a word. At first children crowded around us but then went back to their game, which appeared to involve torturing some kind of insect.

Finally we arrived at a tin shack, which I could hardly believe was someone's home. Joachim knocked on the makeshift door. A face peered out, recognised him and invited us in. Inside there were four children between the ages of two and ten, plus their mother. The floor was beaten earth and the sleeping arrangements consisted of blankets on it. There was no running water. Ramón translated what the mother was telling Joachim: three of the children were ill but they couldn't afford any medicines. Two had sores on their legs, which I had a look at and which seemed quite infected; the other had some heart condition, which caused him to breathe with difficulty. I asked how old they were and Ramón had to repeat their ages because at first I thought I'd misheard – they were all much smaller than you would have expected. The father had abandoned them a few months before. Now the family was dependent on what the children could beg or steal – money, food, or anything they could sell.

Ramón asked me, in English, if I had any medicines in the clinic that I could give them. He wasn't particularly interested in animals and we had never discussed how the clinic ran or the difference between being a vet in England and being a vet in Colombia. I explained that in Colombia the vets were like doctors in England, where the practitioner diagnosed and handed over a prescription, which the pet-owners took to the pharmacist. There was nothing much that I, or any of us, could do, except give them some money and offer sympathy.

As we walked down the mountainside towards the affluent centre I felt sick at heart and all desire to continue working at the clinic evaporated. Across the valley I could make out the ranches of the well-to-do. It was time to move on – either into teaching or home: I hadn't the stomach for the trivia of the mega-rich any more. I would have to talk to Cristina first, I decided, and ultimately Eduardo. It was not something that I looked forward to, because I liked them both.

In veterinary medicine the days you remember are usually the chaotic ones when everything happens at once and you think you'll never get through. But the next day everything seemed to go right. Maybe I was overreacting, I thought, as I surveyed Popeye walking round the room quite well while his mistress, the bright-eyed Isabella, fired questions at me. The family was not rich: hospital doctors in Colombia were paid no more than they are anywhere else, and if I hadn't been around to fix Popeye's smashed leg, he wouldn't be there now. Perhaps I did do some good. Perhaps the mix I had now – half vet, half teacher – was about right.

It had been five weeks since I fixed Popeye's leg. Dr Jaramillo had brought him in because the night before the end of the pin had broken through the skin. Unlike many clients in this situation he didn't panic – he knew that the pin was like the tip of the iceberg and there was little chance of it coming out in the short-term.

Once again, he had starved the cat and turned up unannounced at eight-thirty with Isabella as ever in tow. For a Colombian cat, Popeye was easy-going and he let me feel the leg without protesting – purring, even. There was a good callus in the middle of the bone where the fracture had been, showing that it had healed.

A large section of the pin was now showing, enough for me to get a good purchase on it: I simply grabbed it and gave it a good yank. Popeye merely looked startled and went on purring as the pin came out. 'That's it,' I said to Isabella, who looked equally startled. 'No need for another anaesthetic. He's cured.'

¡Viva El Vet!

The next client, who had just been let in by Cristina, heard these words and laughed. It was Dr Marulanda with Horatio, and Dr Jaramillo turned out to be his boss – which was how Dr Marulanda had come to hear of me. While I looked at Horatio's leg they had a bit of banter about who was going to look after the patients while both surgeons were with the vet.

The pathology report on Horatio's tumour had come back the day before: it was melanoma – one of the most malignant cancers. Dr Marulanda wasn't sure what the prognosis was – humans and animals were different, after all. Normally the prognosis is poor, as the cancer tends to spread rapidly, but here we were, a month after the operation, and there was perfect healing and no sign of any involvement in the lymph nodes. I was cautiously optimistic, but it's not usually a good sign when the growth is between the toes, because it is usually the fast-spreading type of melanoma that occurs there. The fact that there was no sign of recurrence or spread made me think that we were going to be lucky. 'It might be an idea to X-ray his lungs at your hospital,' I said, 'but so far there are no obvious signs of spread. I can't explain why. Some animals seem to recover and not obey the textbooks.'

A familiar toot interrupted our discussion, and Pedro Ramirez arrived at the door. The older doctor recognised him and they shook hands. They evidently moved in the same circles. As I was beginning to learn, Medellín was a small town. Which of his animals was in trouble this time, I wondered, Sasha, Bonita or Rocky the horse?

'I was just passing,' he said, 'and I thought you'd like to know that my wife's horse has won again. That injection worked wonders,' he said, and with a magician's flourish he produced a bottle of whisky. 'This will help with Medellín's cold nights,' he assured me, but I resisted his suggestion to open it and have a drink all round. After all – by Colombian or English time – it was still only eleven o'clock. All three clients left together in good spirits. As indeed was I: by lunchtime we were three hundred pesos better off plus a bottle of whisky – not bad just on check-ups.

With my regular weekly money from the Institute I thought I was rich enough to take Marta out for dinner that evening. I had booked a table at a small restaurant near to her home – she would have to be in by eleven so I didn't want to waste time in getting her back from somewhere further afield. The centre of town had been a hive of activity over the past few days and there was little sign now of the riot. Windows had been repaired, burned-out cars removed and rubble cleared away. Back at the Institute, Dan was recovering – his church had bought him some new Bibles and clothes, and he was his usual thoughtful self, buying me a coffee as I arrived for my teaching stint.

Eating out in a nice restaurant was a relatively rare experience for me in Colombia, but it wasn't going to clean me out – it was still about half the price that a similar meal would have cost me in London.

At first conversation was a bit stilted. I said how much I'd enjoyed meeting her sister, and she told me how much her sister had liked me. The conversation soon drifted on to her family. Her family lived in a village called Concordia, about four hours to the south of Medellín by bus. She went home about once a month, she said, and her next visit was scheduled for the following weekend. How about if I went with her? Sounded good to me. I could stay in her brother's bedroom, she said. He was away at university. So yes, I said, we could go together. We chinked glasses.

The strangest thing had been when I asked for the wine list. After going through it and reckoning that the Chilean red would do nicely, I had asked Marta if that would be all right with her or whether she would prefer white. It turned out she had never drunk a glass of wine in her life. Two glasses later and she was in full flood talking about the *noviazgo*, a word I didn't know but which sounded as if it meant new voyage or new journey, which would fit with her talk of family life. I had happily drunk the rest of the bottle. The local beer and *aguardiente* were all very well, but when it comes to food, nothing can beat a good glass of wine, and although I was getting the gist of what she was saying, the detail passed me by. But I was enjoying the evening: good food, good wine and a beautiful girl. *Noviazgo*? I'll look that one up in the dictionary later, I thought.

Talk about home made me think of England. I told her about Rochester, about Kent, about the Harmsworth. I told her that although I liked her country, England was where I saw my future. She nodded, saying that it wouldn't be a problem – she could come with me.

I wasn't sure how the conversation had taken this turn. I mean, although I gathered I had the thumbs-up from her sister, here she was talking about coming to England, presumably with me.

Her aunt Doña Pepa was waiting up for us and seemed excited about the *noviazgo*, welcoming me into the house for the first time. It was the first ordinary house I had been in: very simple and basic. It was one storey and built, I imagined, of concrete blocks covered in stucco. Unlike terraced houses in England that had a continuous frontage, every other house here was set back, creating a staggered effect. At the centre was a courtyard. Off this was the ablutions area, which was open to the elements so at night you could look up at the stars. On the occasional hot night, Doña Pepa told me, the family would sit out under the stars and talk. There was no television. After a *tinto* and a kiss goodnight – more than usually lingering and passionate – I headed home.

Although Doña Pepa's house was only about half a mile from the clinic I didn't feel entirely comfortable in these streets. It wasn't an area I was familiar with. Then my worst fears were realised. Three suspicious-looking characters were walking towards me. They were young and poorly dressed. I crossed to the other side and they did, too, putting us on a collision course. Should I turn round? If I carried on I was walking into trouble. Planning how to evade violence was becoming a habit. When one was about twenty yards away he looked at me and said, 'You got a light?'

When they rushed me I was ready. I took off like a scalded cat. Never in all those weekends of practice when I was younger had I ever thought that my ability to outrun most people on two legs would end up being so useful.

After about two hundred yards they gave up and I eased down to a jog, turning into my road. The half-mile hadn't taken much more than a couple of minutes and I was glad that I hadn't drunk all of the wine or I might have been less fortunate.

At the Harmsworth I had become used to clients who were poor. In Colombia I had got used to clients with money. But the next day two distinctly impoverished individuals knocked at the door with a German shepherd on an old chain lead. To Cristina's obvious displeasure, I opened the door. The poor dog's head was lolling to one side and its ear was virtually scraping the ground. On closer examination the ear seemed to be caked in something.

I gave up trying to understand what the animal's owners were saying – it seemed to be a dialect of Spanish that I hadn't come across. Cristina kept muttering that they were poor *campesinos*, she called them ignorant, who had done what they thought was best for their dog, which they kept to guard their meagre home in the *tugurios*. They had heard about me after my visit with Ramón and Joachim, and they were sure I would do something for it.

As she listened to their story Cristina raised an eyebrow. For all her fear of *campesinos*, she was a good woman who had a tremendous compassion for animals that she had learned from Eduardo. But she knew – as I did, of course – that we would have to try to sort out the problem with little chance of recompense. It didn't worry me as I was due my weekly visit to Bosun and he could pay for the unfortunate dog that was snarling in front of me.

Five days earlier, it seemed, the dog had cut her ear on the edge of the corrugated iron from which the family home was constructed. They had been unsuccessful in stemming the blood, and had finally resorted to encasing the ear in concrete, which they were using to replace the dirt floor in the home. I had heard a good many stories in my time as a vet, but this was something new. The concrete had set, of course, and the dog would not let anyone near her to try to remove it. I had already decided that discretion was definitely the better part of valour on this occasion. She might have been lopsided with the weight of the concrete pulling her down, but that didn't prevent her trying to maim me. This was a dog who was trained to be vicious, and vicious she most certainly was.

After a struggle, which involved all four of us, Eva – as she was called – was restrained and trussed up ready for an anaesthetic. To solve the problem we had to raid Eduardo's toolbox and find a hammer and chisel.

Bit by bit I chipped off the concrete to reveal a sore-looking ear. This was bathed and dressed with an antiseptic cream and I gave the owners some antibiotics, which we had spare. The next problem was getting her home. With an hour's intravenous anaesthetic she would need at least twenty-four hours' rest. Fortunately the *campesinos* turned out to be amazingly resourceful and had thought of that: they had brought a converted pram with them into which they deposited the still slumbering patient.

'*Muchas gracias*, Doctor,' the older one said, extending his hand and smiling a toothless smile. He brought out two twenty-peso notes to pay me.

I knew this was likely to be a day's income for him so I refused it. 'She'll need some extra food,' I said. 'Spend it on that.' They were both surprised and grateful, and struggled off down the road leaving us to clean up.

I looked at my watch – eleven-thirty. I left Cristina tidying up and went into the sitting room to read the newspaper. When Pilar was around, I gave it a wide berth, but she hadn't been seen for a couple of days so I assumed she would be with Hector.

As I sat there, with my new godson Ian David playing at my feet, I could hardly believe how easily I had adapted to Colombian ways, and the guilt that always hovered about the tiny amount of work I was doing compared with what I accomplished at the Harmsworth was mitigated that morning by having helped a genuinely ill animal belonging to *campesinos* instead of the pampered pets of the rich.

I was vaguely aware of the clinic bell ringing and assumed that Cristina would deal with it. Five minutes later there was a lot of shouting going on, and I went to the window, just in time to see a couple of men legging it down the road. Seconds later Cristina opened the door, looking utterly distraught. 'They've stolen the microscope!' she blurted out. I ran outside and into the road but the two thieves had disappeared.

When Cristina had heard the bell she had gone outside but found nobody there. Just before she turned to go back in, an oldish man on a bicycle stopped and asked her over. She left the parking space in front of the garage and walked to where he was standing in the road.

'How much does it cost for the vaccinations and tail-cutting?' he asked. He got in a couple more questions before she went back inside. It had been enough time. Evidently two accomplices had been hiding behind the door and went in as soon as she went over to the old man. They had taken a couple of hundred pesos – not much was in the till, fortunately – and, much more damagingly, the microscope, Eduardo's pride and joy.

'Shouldn't we call the police?' I suggested naïvely.

I had unwittingly said the only thing that could have made Cristina laugh under the circumstances, which she did. She shook her head.

'I suppose the microscope is insured?'

Cristina didn't know. It seemed that insurance was costly, which was why so many Colombians relied on someone being around all the time to prevent such things happening. If that was the case we had been well and truly stung. But these things happened. And, anyway, something as valuable as that must have been insured, I reckoned. Eduardo wouldn't have been so foolish. I resolved not to worry about it until I'd checked out the insurance situation. In spite of all the commotion I was hungry and when Maria came in to tell me that lunch was ready I sat down and enjoyed a bowl of bean soup.

An hour later, when I was just about to head off to the Institute, the phone rang. Maria answered it. Her eyes flashed wildly. The caller had refused to identify himself but asked if it was true that we were looking for a cheap microscope. She repeated his offer: 'He says one hundred US dollars will secure this magnificent apparatus.'

'Tell him we're not interested,' I said.

A big mistake.

Chapter 15

'You should have bought the microscope back – save you a lot of trouble in the long run,' Ramón said, taking a deep drag on his cigarette, squinting. 'What I mean to say is, will you be able to buy another one for that price?'

I hadn't thought about it like that. The answer was certainly in the negative.

Ramón and I were savouring five minutes of freedom before our next lesson and he couldn't resist a smile when I had told him of the burglars and their *modus operandi*. 'True professionals,' he said, with what might easily have been mistaken for respect. 'You know, Dave,' he added, taking a reflective look at the cigarette, as if calculating how much longer it was going to last, 'Eduardo or his broad will argue that as you were in charge you're responsible for the loss of the microscope. They'll get you locked up,' he went on, grinning at the picture in his mind of my incarceration.

This had to be a wind-up – and a wind-up in extremely bad taste, I reckoned. At the same moment I caught sight of Marta waving at me, and I remembered what I had to ask Ramón. Anyway, a change of subject was definitely called for.

'What does *noviazgo* mean?' I asked.

Ramon made a face as if he had just trodden in dog dirt. '*Noviazgo* is like when you're gonna get married – kind of an engagement.'

My mouth was suddenly drier than a desert.

¡Viva El Vet!

At the same moment he spotted Marta coming towards us. 'You don't mean? Not you two?' he said – a little surprised.

'Er, not exactly.' I hesitated. 'Just that I'm going to see the folks this weekend.'

Ramón opened his mouth and roared. 'That's it, then. You're a condemned man.'

What with the microscope and now this, it was exactly how I felt. I was in it well and truly up to my neck.

Marta slipped her arm through mine after giving me the customary kiss on the cheek that Colombians do all the time. Her class wasn't for another three hours yet, but she had got off early and decided to hang around and talk during the coffee-breaks. She had become very proprietorial and wasn't pleased if any of the other students came over to me. I smiled wanly. Locked up? Engaged?

I felt waves of panic. I had imagined something far less complicated. But then I remembered Marta saying she would like to live in England. And something Ramón had said to me came back: that Marta was the type of Colombian girl who would never leave her homeland and go to England without first being married.

Meeting the folks was a preliminary step.

More waves of panic.

What the hell was I going to do about this weekend? How could I get out of it? Then a calm voice inside me said that I should visit her family so that they could see I was a 'decent' chap who wasn't going to run off with their daughter. Certainly not. That was the last thing on my mind.

Anyway, Concordia sounded exotic and I wanted to see what it was like. Gradually I calmed down and got on with the job of teaching the students that 'there are saints in the church' and how to say that 'there aren't'. It was hardly inspirational on the best of days but Jairo had asked me to use the books. That day my heart definitely wasn't in it.

Four days later I found myself down at the bus station. I had gone to Dõna Pepa's house to pick Marta up and had been greeted effusively – and I was only too aware how often the word *noviazgo* cropped up. It turned out that Doña Pepa was coming with us, presumably to chaperone us on the journey, although if anything untoward was possible on a bus, then my imagination didn't run to it.

So it was three disparate individuals who clambered on board an old-fashioned bus, 1930s vintage, I would guess. Not only did it have the standard no glass in the windows, but the windows doubled as doors. It was more like a bus you might find on a children's roundabout. Everyone climbed through the windows on to the seats, which, all things considered, was practical as the aisle was taken up with bags – everything from traditional suitcases to packages tied with string, hens in wire cages and sacks that I suspected contained unidentifiable animals as from time to time the contents moved.

There was a large roof rack on to which some passengers attached themselves with webbing. This was probably illegal but gave the driver extra money for himself, and maybe, I thought more charitably, an extra incentive to drive slowly and carefully. This soon proved not to be the case. The motto of the bus company was reputed to be 'better never to arrive than to arrive late' and I soon found out that there was more than an element of truth in that.

The rot set in early. We tore up the main road south out of town at sixty miles an hour, which felt like a hundred. I wondered how the *campesinos* on the roof were faring. Whenever we slowed down I leaned out to look, but all I could see was impassive shapes wrapped in ponchos against the wind. Soon we began to climb winding mountain roads, and I realised we were going to be even higher than Medellín.

Bizarrely, the only place where I ever found that Colombian time was not the norm was on that bus: we arrived in Concordia exactly four hours later. As always, I found the scenery fascinating. Marta had been happy to let me sit by the window. In her eyes this was a dangerous seat and my offering to do so was the equivalent of walking on the kerb side of a pavement.

Concordia was delightful, with almost Alpine scenery. We arrived in mid-afternoon and there was already a chill in the air. The village was like any other mountain village I had ever come across, except for an impossibly large church – almost a cathedral in size. The streets that fanned out from the central square were cobbled and steep. Transport was by horse or foot. The whole place seemed timeless. As we began our climb towards the family home I noted a vast statue of Christ, with arms outstretched, that dominated the valley, and tried to imagine the work involved in building it so high up. It was certainly impressive.

'Can you go up there?' I asked Marta, pointing to the Christ figure. The elderly Doña Pepa was scurrying up the impossibly steep street in front of us.

'Of course, David. You want to go? There is a wonderful view of the Andes and, of course, the village.'

'Perhaps later,' I said, rather lamely. I might have thought I was conditioned to the altitude after nearly six months in Medellín but I obviously wasn't: I was quite puffed already. Thank goodness all I had brought was a small hold-all. If any brigands tried to get one over on me here I might as well hand it over straight away and avoid any further fuss.

As we made our way up the village, women called greetings to Marta and her aunt, and you didn't need a degree in Spanish to tell that I was being given the once-over. It was like walking up the aisle. The idea, once there, multiplied and soon my head was ringing with 'Here Comes The Bride'.

The family house lay towards the edge of the village and by the time we arrived a reception committee had assembled, although how many were family and how many were just curious about the *novio*, I never discovered.

That was how I was described. *Novio*. Betrothed.

The house was one of the bigger ones in the village and had been in the family ever since anyone could remember. It was wooden and at the side there was an upstairs extension supported on stilts. The garden at the side was incredible. It was here that everyone stood for the formal introductions. It was a mass of tropical flowers, colours that shouldn't go together but somehow did – orange, purple, red, pink. We sat on some rustic seats that Marta's father had made. He was called Octavo because he was the eighth child in his family, Marta explained.

In fairly rapid succession I was introduced to her father and mother, a granny, a couple of aunts, one of whom was a nun, an uncle, two younger brothers and three sisters, all of whom I think were older, not to mention several of the neighbours.

Octavo hugged his daughter with a look of anguish. Almost instinctively I could tell what was going through his mind: he was about to lose her. Oh, no, he wasn't. Granny stared impassively at me as though I was from Mars, which for all the contrast between London and Concordia, I might as well have been.

Once the formalities were over it was straight to the

jugular. The nun kicked off the proceedings. First on the agenda? Religion, naturally. I was Protestant, she had heard. Was that true? For the present purposes it would do, I decided. Did Protestants believe in Jesus Christ? Did we take communion? What about confession? And so on and so forth. It was a latter day Inquisition. Religious studies had never been a strong point at school – I distinguished myself by getting 14 per cent in an exam shortly before it was decided that O-level RE probably wasn't a good idea. It wasn't that I was a heathen, but mine had never been a religious family and church attendances were few and far between.

As the questions came thick and fast I decided that smiling and nodding was probably the best policy. Then came a question that needed a concrete answer. Would I go to church tomorrow? It was Sunday. I nodded, everyone seemed happy and we relaxed.

The family had a couple of maids, and Marta told them to get us some coffee, in a perfectly civilised way. But, once again, I felt uncomfortable that these women were effectively slaves. Even though I should have got used to it with the way Maria was treated by Eduardo and especially Pilar, I still found it immensely distasteful. With Maria I could try at least to show what I felt, but here, with Marta's family, I could do nothing. With a jolt like a cartoon lightning flash I realised that Marta would never settle in England and I would never settle in Colombia: the gulf was just too great.

It was extraordinary. At once the panic waves stopped and I resolved to be as nice to her as I could, but she would have to be told, and sooner rather than later. But my relief was enormous.

We had dinner at around six. I wasn't used to huge family

gatherings: the largest my family ran to was at Christmas – just the folks and my sister. That evening Octavo sat at the head of a large table with all his family around him and his wife Martha at the other end. The maids brought in some kind of lamb stew and rice with salad. As usual we drank milk and grace was said. It was like being in a time warp: grace had been said here in this way ever since Christianity arrived with Christopher Columbus.

Nobody had television because the reception wasn't good, so the evening was spent in telling stories, jokes and general banter. The journey, the Inquisition and the strain of keeping up with the conversation had taken its toll, and I was glad when Doña Pepa and Marta showed me my room at not much after nine. With a smile that was positively treacly, Doña Pepa motioned to the two of us to say goodnight in front of the door. We had about thirty seconds, but even so I imagined Doña Pepa lurking down the corridor.

My bedroom looked out towards the mountains, but as the window didn't have glass I fell asleep to the sounds of the village in full Saturday-night festive mode: people in bars laughing, dogs barking, and downstairs I had no doubt that the virtues and otherwise of the gringo were fully discussed.

I was woken the next morning by church bells summoning the faithful to the first service. The view out of the window, the morning sun having only just risen over the mountain peaks, was stunning. My first thought was that this was paradise, and why on earth would anyone want to leave it to live in one of the world's most overpopulated, dirty, dangerous cities, as Marta did.

Later, as we trooped into church, her reasons became clearer. Although there were a few younger couples with half a dozen kids each, the bulk of the congregation consisted of old people, some of whom were very old. There was something about the Andean air, Octavo told me. It was very pure and life was very healthy and 'sane': the men in his family had always lived into their nineties.

It was many years since he had left the village and he had no intention of ever doing so again. With the family owning the big old house he only needed to work to eat. His job as a carpenter and odd-job man fed everyone well. Marta was now self-sufficient and he had several brothers who had done well in life and were able to help with his children's education. Antioquian people prided themselves on having large families and I could see that it might work to the advantage of the family, with the well-off ones happy to help out the less well-off.

We had arrived at the church a few minutes late. Although the village was small and the church huge, it was full to overflowing. I felt like a giant among the villagers, most of whom were a good deal smaller than I. I stood at the back, with a good view of the priest and the altar. Looking at him I wondered which category of Colombian priesthood he fitted – the lady-killer or the left-wing revolutionary. I could just about follow the Spanish and several village girls were having their first communion. This added considerably to the length of the service but they looked angelic in their frothy white dresses.

As we left, some of Marta's brothers manoeuvred me to a bar by the square. Half of the village was out drinking. The male half: the female half were busying themselves with Sunday lunch. Marta gave me a wave and went off back up the hill. It no longer surprised me. South America is still famed for its machismo: the cult of the male-dominated society.

And it has to be said that – athlete and beer-drinker as I am – I am not averse to a bit of male-only society myself from time to time. I looked at them with something approaching envy. Everyone seemed so at ease with themselves and each other. Could I become one of them? I might easily have been seduced into this lifestyle. But what could I do here?

That line of thought never got past the starting grid. Although there was farming going on, it looked fairly basic, subsistence level. Only the presence of polythene tunnels outside the village showed that things had moved on since the land was first settled. Mostly they lived on the income from coffee and money sent back from children making their way in the big city.

About twenty minutes later Octavo arrived – he had been talking to the priest about some repairs needed to the bell-tower. Over the next half-hour he tried to get out of me in a roundabout way what my intentions were. So I told him what I had told no one else and what I had only recently admitted to myself: that I would soon be going back to England, even though at the moment I didn't have a job to go to. I omitted to add that getting a job would be easy. I decided to pre-empt any questions about an engagement by telling him that Marta and I were 'just friends'.

He relaxed visibly and bought me another beer. Then, after I had downed it quickly, we were off for a picnic lunch in the garden. Something must have been said because Marta and I were allowed to climb up to the statue of Christ alone after lunch. In any case the trek would have defeated all of the others, with the possible exception of Octavo. It was steep and at this altitude – about six thousand feet – hard work. But, as Marta had promised, the view at the top was worth the hour's climb.

The village nestled in a hollow in the mountains, which

completely surrounded it. The mountains seemed so close – almost on top of us. A single road came up from a valley miles below and I could see it winding down and down – a clear view of around thirty miles, I guessed.

'Why did you leave this?' I asked her, after we had stood there not saying a word, just drinking in the beauty of the land.

'No job, and the men, they are all *machistas*,' she said, wrinkling her nose in contempt.

'You don't include your father in that?'

'Well, he is not so bad. But there are six children and my mother is only forty.'

This surprised me as she looked quite a bit older than that.

'What kind of a life is it?' Marta continued. 'And look at how it has left her.' '*Robusta*', was how she put it, but meaning that she was well overweight. 'I do not want children,' said Marta. We had never talked about such things before – that would indeed have set my alarm bells ringing. But I was taken aback: a Colombian woman who didn't want children?

I didn't pursue the subject as I felt it would inevitably lead to talk of marriage. It wasn't that the idea of marriage to Marta was something I hadn't thought about – I had. But I knew my future didn't lie in Colombia and that Marta would not be happy in England.

We walked down in silence to the family home where preparations were being made for our departure. The bus left at four in the afternoon with an arrival time of eight – early enough to minimise the dangers of being out and about. Bus robberies had been occurring quite frequently but mainly on night buses, especially the inter-city ones. Ours would not be a prime target.

David Grant

I was sad when I said goodbye to the family. Everyone was saying, 'See you again soon,' and I heard myself repeating the same phrases. They were such good, honest people and I doubted – correctly, as it turned out – that I would see them again.

On the journey back to Medellín Marta dozed, while I pondered how I was to tackle the subject of leaving Colombia on my own. The more I looked at the extraordinary scenery of the Andes the more it hammered home to me how much I missed my own country, the people, the pubs, even the weather. I longed for long winter days – even foggy days. By the time the bus arrived in Medellín, I had made up my mind. I would stay only a couple of months more at the most. I would do my best in the clinic until then, and in the meantime visit Eduardo in Apartado to tell him so that he could sort something out.

Maybe, I thought, Pilar would leave the house to live with Hector, and Eduardo would be free to take over the clinic again. I knew that if she continued to live there, Eduardo could never come back. Perhaps I should encourage her relationship with Hector more than I had previously. How complicated life is, I thought.

But my time in Colombia had not been wasted even if it hadn't worked out quite as I expected. But, there again, what had I expected? Working in the clinic had done me a lot of good and focused my mind on what I wanted to do with my profession for the next thirty years. Working for the mega-rich was out, however lucrative it might be. No, I would do a spell in private small-animal practice in England for the experience and then – if they'd have me – I'd go back to the RSPCA. I had never been happier than at the Harmsworth. I relaxed at the thought that I would be going back sometime soon, and smiled to myself.

'What are you thinking?' said Marta, when she woke up, leaning against me in the back seat with Doña Pepa on her other side.

'My family.'

'Who in your family?'

'Our dog Judy. I miss her.'

'A dog?' she said, with a laugh. That was another thing: Marta showed no affinity with animals; she was frightened, if anything, of dogs.

'In England many families have a dog,' I explained, 'and they are treated as one of the family.'

This was incomprehensible to her. I sensed she might be spoiling for a fight. Perhaps her father had told her how relieved he was that we were 'just friends'. But I decided not to rise to it. I was tired, and in any case I had a rare busy clinic the next day.

Cristina had booked in a couple of cat spays and cat castrates, plus several vaccinations. What with the Colombian determination to get their money's worth, what would take an hour in England might last a morning.

We arrived at eight and, after a hurried kiss, Doña Pepa and Marta sped off in a taxi while I decided to walk home. I needed to think, and an inherent meanness in spending money on taxis, which exists to this day, persuaded me to take the risk. There was no doubt that, having survived several escapades, I was getting cocky.

The walk did me good. I had everything mapped out now, and I resolved to have as much fun as I could in the time I had left in Colombia. Feeling refreshed and relaxed, I arrived safely at the clinic to find Hector and Pilar waiting for me.

Any ideas I might have had about encouraging their relationship were swiftly dispelled. The expressions on their faces told me that I wasn't about to be invited out to a salsa club. The golden smile that I had fondly imagined was near permanent on Hector's face had been replaced by a calm menacing stare.

'Maria, *tinto*,' Pilar barked. Her expression made her look even less appealing than usual.

Maria hurried in with three black coffees and gave me the faintest of smiles before scuttling back to her quarters.

Hector waited until he heard her door close. Then he cut to the chase. 'The matter of the apparatus,' he began, rather pompously. I was struck suddenly by how coarse his features were. His apparent handsomeness was bolstered by his handmade suits, expensive jewellery and a tan. Behind the façade lurked a much more ordinary-looking man.

'Apparatus?' I replied, playing the innocent.

'The microscope,' said Pilar, through gritted teeth, conveying anger, contempt and pity all in one word.

Hector went on in a tired measured tone such as you might use with a miscreant child, 'Precisely, *amor*.' Here his features softened as he patted his inamorata's bony knee. As he went on he pulled his knuckles one by one, making them crack loudly. I realised that this was one of his habits and I watched, fascinated, as he half dislocated each finger while he thought about his words. 'Dr Serrano's microscope is worth two hundred dollars. This sum is owed to me personally and I expect it to be paid in, shall we say, the reasonably near future? I do not wish to involve my friend in this trivial matter,' and here he mentioned a high-up official in the DAS whom he had mentioned before and who, he had indicated, he had in his pocket.

I nearly laughed thinking of Hector having high-up friends in the DAS, but thankfully managed to stop myself.

'I can assure you that no man cheats me without some regret,' he added, cracking another finger.

¡Viva El Vet!

This episode had taken me by surprise. How Hector found the nerve to imply that I owed the money to him I couldn't imagine.

'Well, I will need some time to lay my hands on that kind of money,' I lied. 'Write home to England – that sort of thing.' I smiled at him nervously. But the smile was not returned.

'Two months – I cannot be more reasonable. I will not speak to you on this matter again.'

He patted his jacket pocket as if to assure himself that his revolver was in place, staring at me meaningfully. 'You understand?' I nodded, and without a word they left to go out. I sat perfectly still with my heart thumping.

Maria came in as soon as she heard the door close, and asked me if I wanted anything to eat.

'No, thanks,' I replied. It was a drink I needed. Two months. That had certainly concentrated my mind.

Chapter 16

Two hundred dollars. Today's equivalent would be about a thousand pounds. What was the alternative? A bullet somewhere in my body. I didn't know what good it would serve anyone, but it only took a quick scan of *El Colombiano* to see that such punishments were meted out without any seeming advantage to anyone. Logic wasn't part of the calculation.

If I had doubled my teaching hours, if I sacrificed my integrity and said yes to ear-cropping and the like, it might just have been possible. But why should I? I hadn't done anything wrong. I wasn't part of a conspiracy to steal the damn thing. If I'd had anything to do with it, the microscope would have been insured. Naïve as I was, I knew about insurance: it's the business equivalent of vaccination.

The sight of Pilar's face only made me more determined to avoid paying. Years later I saw a production of *Macbeth* and felt the hairs rise on my neck when Lady Macbeth came on. It was Pilar. From the first time I had set eyes on her I had never understood how Eduardo had ever been dragged up the aisle by that woman. I suppose once she had got her teeth into him she was just too much of a match for him, which was why he drank. It was the only way out. Divorce in a Catholic country is always difficult and expensive.

That night, lying in my room not yards from my persecutor, I considered my options. In a couple of months I would have been at the clinic for nearly a year. In many ways, time had flown by. Although I'd crammed in a lot, Colombia was such

¡Viva El Vet!

an amazingly diverse country there were still so many places I had not yet seen. I would have liked to stay longer but the obvious way to get out of this situation with my life and manhood intact was to leave. But I would have to tell Eduardo – and that would mean a trip to Apartado.

The next morning we were comparatively busy, if three vaccinations and a cat spay can be called busy. The cat spay was a first for me in Colombia and Cristina had seen few done. My patient, a tortoiseshell, had had many litters and had gradually become part of the family. After the umpteenth batch of kittens the grandmother, a feisty *señora* of about eighty, had decided to resolve the matter. It was she who turned up at eleven-thirty just as I was saying goodbye to the previous client. She got out of a taxi and rang the bell with the cat in a hold-all – like a ferret in a sack. This had not put the animal in a particularly good mood and I had to give her a hefty jab of tranquilliser before thinking about any anaesthetic. Granny announced her intention of staying until the cat was ready to go home – she had contracted the taxi driver for the morning, as the family knew him.

Old ladies, it seemed, did not consider taxi drivers safe. Abuela, as Cristina called her – Spanish for Granny – reminded me of Marta's grandmother: large, formidable and knowing exactly what she wanted. I was surprised to find out that nobody had got round to naming the cat, which would never have happened in England. Although the old *señora* feigned indifference, the cat had clearly wheedled its way into her affections. She was obviously a widow, dressed in black, and like old ladies everywhere, I decided, was probably lacking in human companionship. A cat has the great advantage of not needing much looking after. Faced with a blank space in Cristina's card-index system I decided to give her a name: Lolly, I decided, after a subject that was

very much on my mind. The sum of two hundred pesos –
only just over a dollar – had been agreed with Abuela. Only
$199 to go, then.

Using the last of my cat intravenous anaesthetic imported
from England, Cristina and I managed to get Lolly off to
sleep. Once she had been fastened to the operating table
I began to clip her flank. Flank spays were and still are
routine in England. I had forgotten that most other countries,
America, Spain and apparently Colombia too, preferred to
operate via an incision in the midline of the abdomen. Cristina
tried to stop me but it was too late. 'Eh, *ave Maria, muy feo*,'
very ugly, she muttered.

'Maybe,' I said, undeterred, still clipping away, 'but this
is much safer. If the wound breaks down it will be easy to
fix with no danger to the cat.' The consequences of a wound
breakdown in the midline were awful to contemplate: not to
put too fine a point on it, the guts might spill out.

The operation went smoothly and in fifteen minutes Lolly
was coming round nicely. Abuela popped her head in from
the consulting room to see her pet.

I smiled, said that the operation had gone well and that in
a while she could take her cat home.

To say that her reaction was over the top is an understate-
ment. She took one look, then leaned her head against the
wall, sobbed, then flung herself over the semi-conscious cat
before turning on me with a crazed look in her eyes. I had
never seen such a transformation. The charming old lady had
turned into a deranged witch.

'Murderer! She will die! The hair will never grow back!'
On and on she went. Cristina just shook her hands and gave
me a wild look. These histrionics went on for a good five
minutes. Meanwhile, I tried to explain that the hair *would*
grow back and that in ten days the stitches would come out

and Lolly would be racing about as if nothing had happened, but I was talking to a stone wall.

Eventually Abuela picked up the cat, put her in the hold-all and walked out. The tone of her voice had now changed from grief to fury: 'If you think I am going to pay for such barbarity, you are very much mistaken,' she said, as she swept out to the waiting taxi.

I was totally wrongfooted. This was a first no-payment and dissatisfied client. I couldn't remember a more vociferous one even at the Harmsworth, where some of the clients were not slow in coming forward when unhappy with the treatment. Cristina shrugged her shoulders in an I-told-you-so fashion.

Thank goodness for the three vaccinations we had done beforehand – at least the income would cover the day's costs. My target figure of two hundred dollars was becoming increasingly unrealistic by the hour.

It was a decidedly disconsolate young gringo who got on to the bus that afternoon. But by the time I arrived and saw the usual gang of *gamines* hanging around the bus stop in front of the school, my mood had changed. I was angry. They were just kids, kids with no parents and no one to care for them. No prospects, except a life of prostitution or crime. And an old woman, whose black dress was probably made of silk, was raising the roof because her pet cat had had some fur clipped off her flank. Fuelled by this anger and convinced now that the chances of my paying off Hector were not only remote but non-existent, I decided to take the only other course of action open to me. No more thinking about it. No more prevaricating. Lest the moment should go, I spoke to Jairo and explained that I had run into a spot of trouble at the clinic and that I might be returning to London in the next month or so.

'What sort of trouble?' was his response.

'Too complicated to explain, Jairo.'

His response was to raise my salary by 50 per cent – but that would still not be enough to pay for food and accommodation. Not to mention the impossible task of avoiding Hector's retribution.

Ramón would know how seriously I should take these threats, I decided. At break I told him what had happened. He rubbed the heel of his hand over his chin, which was already showing a five o'clock shadow. 'That guy could get you hurt, no mistake,' were his encouraging words.

Then, as if the answer was all too clear, he added, 'You wanna buy a suit before you go? I can get you a real fine one for ten bucks, straight off the production line.'

Off the back of a lorry, more likely. 'OK,' I said. My God, this was the same black economy that had caused me the problem with the microscope in the first place. I was fast becoming a Colombian. But it made sense: back in London I would need a smart suit for interviews. I had lost five kilos and the old one at home would hang on me as if I was a scarecrow. When in Rome . . .

'Five bucks or four hundred pesos up front now and the rest on delivery,' Ramón continued. He wasted no time. I fished out four hundred pesos.

'That's a bad rate of exchange,' I said. 'Four hundred, and you buy me a *frijoles con chicharron* and a beer.' Bean stew with pork crackling was a simple but filling cheap meal and I was hungry.

Ramón considered this. 'Where's Marta?' he said, playing for time.

'We're having a little misunderstanding.'

In fact, it was more than that. I had told her that I didn't think she would be happy in England, my family was so different from hers and I didn't think she could adapt. She believed she could, I believed she couldn't. But I didn't want to go into all that with Ramón.

'About getting married?' Ramón raised a quizzical eyebrow.

'You could say that. She wants to and I don't, basically,' I said.

Ramón lit another cigarette and took a long, slow drag. 'No way she'll settle in London,' he said. 'She's a *paisa* – family first. You'd have to live here.'

'I know,' I said. 'I'd worked that one out for myself.'

I hadn't seen him since my trip to Concordia and the grilling from the nun. He laughed when I described the scene. 'And of course you realise you'd have to become a Catholic. You like children? Marta is, what, twenty? Let me see, *amigo*,' and he started counting on his fingers, 'how do you feel about raising a family of six or more kids?'

I felt decidedly negative.

What was so strange to me that, far from being understanding – guys together in adversity – Ramón just shrugged. To him these matters were straightforward. Marta and girls like her were for marrying. If I wasn't ready for it I should chase a piece of tail instead. 'We could make a start tonight,' he said, warming to his subject. 'It won't cost you much – a hundred pesos and, trust me, a new woman will make you feel like a new man.'

I didn't want to feel like Ramón's type of new man. I was quite happy with the old one. I made my excuses and went home. An evening with Ian David and Maria seemed infinitely preferable to trawling around a few bars in search of 'fun'.

I left the Institute feeling utterly exhausted. I looked around as I opened the door to the street, seeing the place with fresh eyes: it was no longer where I worked, it was somewhere I would soon be leaving. But, strangely, knowing that I wouldn't be staying much longer didn't make me any happier.

The next thing to do was to tell Eduardo. I couldn't just leave him in the lurch. I called him, didn't tell him why I was coming to Apartado and he didn't ask. He just sounded delighted that I was going up there. I began to feel like a criminal. Now that I had made my decision I wanted to get the whole thing over quickly, but he suggested I wait until a local *fiesta* in a nearby village called San Pedro, famous, apparently, for its *corraleja* – a kind of bullfight, except that the bulls rarely got killed, and then only thanks to an intrepid local youth who got too brave or foolhardy.

I had read about these *fiestas*, which went on for days sometimes in a state of drunken debauchery. It would be another experience, and as things had quietened down since I had given Pilar the impression that I was getting her blood-money organised, life at the clinic had settled into a dull routine. A few weeks more wouldn't hurt and, if anything, my continued presence would lull Hector and his moll into a state of inertia.

It was about a month later that I took five days off and made my way to the airport. Things were tense with Marta – she had already missed a couple of her classes, something she had never done before.

The sight of the plane that was going to transport me to the jungle cheered me up. It was a small ten-seater turbo prop. The flight was magical – low for most of the hour-long journey, apart from the first fifteen minutes when we flew up the valley and went over the ring of mountains that surrounded Medellín.

After half an hour we started descending and I could see the pilots working in the cabin, as the door separating us from them refused to shut. There were two: one, a man in his fifties, spent the entire flight reading a newspaper and smoking; the much younger co-pilot did all the work. For half an hour we flew over impenetrable jungle then suddenly, through the cockpit window, I saw a clearing in the dense foliage. The runway. Without any word to the cabin from the pilots we headed straight for it and I had a fantastic view of the landing. As soon as we were down a jeep appeared, the doors were opened and there, standing on the Tarmac, was Eduardo, looking plumper than before, attired in tropical clothes with a large Panama hat.

'*Bienvenido*, welcome to Apartado,' he said, giving my arm a violent shake. He was in a good humour. 'First we go home. We have time for a beer, and then we must go to San Pedro.'

I was startled. The *fiesta* wasn't till tomorrow. Leave already, for this nearby village?

'But how far is it?' I said.

'About five hours in a jeep – don't worry,' he added, seeing the expression on my face, 'I've arranged transport.'

Getting off the plane was like stepping into a sauna. It must have been over 40°C and humid with it. Before I had walked the thirty yards to where Eduardo had parked his Renault, I was drenched in sweat. I had known it was going to be hot, but this was like a cauldron.

Apartado was a one-street town with dozens of bars and a solitary church. Most of the cars were jeeps or four-wheel drives of some description, with just as many horses tethered outside the bars. The place looked like a film set.

Eduardo lived in a small, unassuming bungalow on the outskirts. There was no air-conditioning, just a fan in each of the two bedrooms. At least he had a fridge, and the ice-cold beer went down well while he outlined his plans. Two of the town's notables – the doctor and the mayor – were picking us up in an hour and we would head off for San Pedro, aiming to reach there by nightfall. The mayor had a *finca* in the village where we were going to stay for a couple of nights during the festivities. We would have one night to enjoy whatever Apartado had to offer before I caught the flight back to Medellín.

I began to relax. My plan had been to tell Eduardo immediately of my imminent departure, but it seemed a shame to spoil his good mood – I had never seen him so animated. The fact that I might be tired after my journey had clearly not occurred to him. But any thoughts I might have had about nodding off on the way to San Pedro were dispelled after a couple of miles when the tarmacked road was replaced by a dirt track with more holes than my well-worn socks.

'Just as well it isn't the rainy season,' Eduardo said cheerily, 'or we'd never be able to make the journey – this would all be mud.'

'When does the rainy season start?' I ventured, thinking of being stuck in San Pedro.

'Not for a few weeks. That's why it's good you're here now,' replied Eduardo, taking a hefty swig out of his *aguardiente* bottle before offering it to the doctor, who was driving, and the mayor, both of whom appeared to be about my age.

They both took equally hefty swigs before it was my turn. Not wishing to be rude I swallowed a good gulp, spluttering as the firewater hit my gullet. This caused much amusement and I realised that my liver was going to suffer over the next few days. The jeep was open-top and I glimpsed tropical birds and occasional monkeys as we trundled on, seemingly interminably. Five hours is long even in English time. On a dirt track, in 40°C with *aguardiente*, it is endless.

¡Viva El Vet!

As the alcohol took effect, the driver took less and less care to avoid the potholes and we bounced about. It was worse for us in the back and several times I had to hang on for grim death to avoid being ejected on to the track. Another bottle of *aguardiente* appeared. Inwardly I cursed: at this rate I would be unconscious by the time we got to San Pedro. Then, suddenly, we rounded a bend and a solitary notice proclaimed we had arrived.

Almost immediately we swung into a simple *finca* along-side a rustic, open-air, restaurant. We piled out and show-ered. There was only cold water but that hardly mattered when the temperature was in the middle forties and it was very humid. With clean clothes on and feeling mightily refreshed we sat down to have a meal. There were a few lights in the restaurant and the constant churning noise coming from the direction of the kitchens told me the electricity was supplied by a generator. The *finca* we were staying in had the same system, as did a couple of lively bars in the main square. Otherwise it was candles. It reminded me of the Harmsworth during the three-day week.

I ordered a *sancocho de gallina*, the chicken stew. 'There will be a delay of perhaps half an hour,' said the owner apologetically.

'*No importa*,' I said, reflecting that my stomach could do with a rest after bumping about for five hours.

Minutes later a cacophony of sound interrupted our con-versation. It sounded like a chicken trying to evade capture. Feathers flying from behind a fence at the back of the restaurant shortly confirmed this diagnosis.

'You have chosen wisely,' said Dr Gutierrez, surprisingly clear-headed after driving with so much alcohol inside him. 'The chicken will be fresh.'

For a second I was tempted to change my mind. But at

exactly that moment the squawking stopped. The chicken was now an ex-chicken. Also smells from the kitchen were wafting my way, hunger had set in and I dismissed it from my mind as we got on to the subject of the festivities.

Apparently every year at this time three days were given over to an orgy of drunken debauchery prior to the coming of the rainy season. The main attraction would be the *corraleja*, the running of the bulls, followed by an all-night dance to live bands. The next day there would be a service in the village church followed by more drinking, dancing, gambling, cock-fighting and anything else that could be arranged. People for miles around would come and the population of a thousand or so would swell to four or five times that. Only Sincelejo, a much bigger town to the north of us and nearer to the Caribbean coast, was more famous for its annual *fiesta* and *corraleja* in January.

The chicken duly arrived and went down well with another beer. Suddenly extreme tiredness hit me. By now Eduardo was drunk and expansive. 'Tomorrow,' he said, clapping me on the shoulder, 'we must talk about the *plata* for the clinic.'

My stomach lurched. Now I understood the reason for his good humour. Not only did he not know that I was planning to leave the country, he assumed that my visit was to agree a price for me to buy the practice from him.

I swallowed. 'Fine,' I said.

'And don't worry about this,' he added, brandishing some notes and ordering another bottle. He did it with the air of a man who had just won the lottery. But that didn't make me feel any more guilty. The meal was ridiculously cheap.

A few minutes later I climbed through the mosquito netting and collapsed into a deep sleep. At least the *aguardiente* had prevented me lying awake all night worrying. The talk about the *plata* would wait till morning.

Chapter 17

I slept surprisingly well and woke early. Snores from the other rooms told their own story. It would be an hour or two before the others surfaced, I reckoned. I had woken briefly at about two when I'd heard them crashing about, obviously the worse for wear.

I felt just a little smug as I showered, dressed and went out to explore. It was just after seven-thirty and there was little sign of life. Already the temperature was soaring and there wasn't a cloud in the sky. The village consisted of a square with a couple of bars and restaurants. Four main tracks fanned out from the square and various streets intersected the main roads. There were a few jeeps but otherwise no cars. The houses were simple one-storey wooden affairs, but the effect was charming and it felt safe. It was possible to walk round the village in half an hour, and on the outskirts I came across a gang of men building a large corral almost the size of a football pitch. The walls were some fifteen feet high and in front was a terrace of seats. Behind, in a fenced-off field, I could see some unusual-looking cattle: huge white bulls with a prominent hump that rose up like a hill behind their heads. They looked a bit like Charolais bulls, except for the hump. I asked one of the workmen what type of cattle they were.

'*Cebu*,' he replied. '*Muy feroz.*' I looked closely at them – I was now in vet mode. They looked peaceful enough, grazing on the unfamiliar-looking grass. I was near enough to see that a couple of them were covered in ticks on their shoulders, but apart from that they were in good condition.

Back in tourist mode I headed for the square and found one of the bars already open. Breakfast in the open air – coffee and fried bananas – had never tasted better and I returned to the mayor's house in good humour.

By now it was nine and a steady stream of vehicles and people on horseback announced the start of festivities. The house was still quiet and nobody was awake. A hammock in the garden slung between a couple of trees looked inviting. In no time at all I was asleep and was astonished when Eduardo shook me awake at eleven.

The village had come to life and a *campesino* band had started playing in the main square. I recognised the rhythm of the *cumbia* – a Colombian national dance. The musicians were perfectly in tune and the urge to dance was almost irresistible. For the first time in weeks I missed Marta: she might not like animals but she could dance.

Eduardo had lost none of the previous day's good humour. Over the first of the day's beers he told me that his divorce was now going through. I thought again of the advice Gloria had given me: Colombia is full of paradoxes. And it was: extreme wealth and extreme poverty; children dying and people worrying whether their dogs' ears were straight; fat priests stepping over emaciated beggars; good Catholics not thinking twice about getting a divorce. From the grilling I had received from the nun, to Ramón's politico uncle and the stories I'd heard generally about priests using their cassocks as a disguise for serial philandering, Catholicism in Colombia was definitely a paradox. Not that Eduardo – or Pilar, for that matter – had ever shown the remotest interest in religion.

I was deep in my thoughts and admiring a fine-looking horse. Like the Cebu bulls he was huge, a bay with a white stripe down his nose. He stood calmly as the cacophony of hundreds of (mainly) men getting drunk increased steadily. I had now accepted the first *aguardiente* and was wondering how to avoid drinking too many of them when an opportunity presented itself. The owner of the horse, who was deep in conversation with Eduardo – a client, perhaps, or potential client – noticed me casting an appreciative eye over his horse. 'His name is Danger,' he said, which, because it was pronounced 'Dan-hair', took me a minute or two to work out. 'You like Danger?'

'He's a beautiful horse,' I admitted.

'Take him for a ride round the village,' he said, with an expansive gesture. 'He's getting bored.'

The effect of two beers and one *aguardiente* was enough for me to suspend my natural caution. Besides, this was macho land: I would look foolish and maybe insult the man if I refused his offer. I climbed up the fence and gingerly eased myself on to Danger's immense back. I leaned forward and untethered him. A gentle squeeze of his flanks was all it took and he was off down the road, trotting in a very stylish way – he had obviously been schooled. As we left the square I heard his owner's voice ringing in my ears. 'Careful with the mares.' He laughed, and made a strange hand signal.

No wonder Danger was so big: he was a fully fledged stallion. I pulled on the reins gently and he eased from his trot to a walk. I hadn't been on a horse of this size and power since I was a student about seven years before. When I had ridden at Bertica's parents' *finca* my mount had been a gentle mare nearing retirement. But I soon relaxed and enjoyed the view from a good eight feet up. I looked round nervously but there was no one else on horseback: they were all in the bars or out and about on foot. Danger and I walked on and I heard some frantic shouting – maybe a local football match,

I thought, and ambled up to see. I came to a fenced-off area, which was banked on all sides, and filled with men yelling themselves hoarse. I got to the back of the crowd and saw something I had only read about: a cockfight. It was a pretty barbarous business with each adversary circling the other then wading in with murderous attacks with their talons to which were attached spurs to maximise injury. The shouting reminded me of a seedy greyhound track where I had once had the misfortune to act as the vet on duty. The excitement, I soon discovered, was caused not by the fight itself but by the betting. I reckoned that every man watching this cruel spectacle had money on one of the cockerels.

A great shout went up as one of the birds got the upper hand and was furiously pecking at the other which was now on the ground. The loser was dying, and the victor stood on top of him occasionally pecking viciously at his face. A man in front of me threw his hat to the ground in disgust. I, too, felt disgust, but for different reasons: the man wasn't interested in the barbarity of what was happening, just angry at having lost money.

This was the moment when Danger chose to lift his tail and shed about half a ton of manure. It virtually buried the man's hat. I moved on, hoping that the loser was too drunk to notice what had happened to his hat before he put it back on. I didn't hang around to find out and we trotted back to the corral, which was finished. 'What time does it start?' I asked one of the spectators, who were taking their seats.

'At four.' Another hour.

I squeezed Danger's flanks again and we trotted out of town into the jungle. I saw toucans, parrots and monkeys that turned to chatter at me – as though they had never seen a huge horse with a man perched precariously on its back.

And exactly how precarious I was soon to find out. As I

turned the mighty animal back to the village, he took this as a signal to gallop. All pretence of riding vanished, I simply hung on for my life. As we arrived in the square, Danger came to an abrupt stop at the bar and I half fell off, but landed on my feet, in front of Eduardo and his friends. They seemed impressed by my horsemanship, thinking that I had dismounted with a flourish instead of the shambles that it had been.

'The *corraleja* starts at four,' I announced. Leaving Danger in the custody of the bar owner, we set off for the corral. We had got the last seats at the front – everyone else would have to stand or sit on the wooden walls. A few thousand people rapidly filled the arena and the band turned up to entertain us prior to the running of the bulls. I didn't know what to expect, but having seen cockfighting – and stone cold sober in comparison to everyone else – I didn't feel comfortable. Maybe I would need to check out Danger later. I had got really attached to that horse.

My thoughts were interrupted by a blast on a trumpet. An even louder shout than I had heard from the cockfight spectators went up. A huge Cebu bull charged in. He was in an irritated mood and stood still for a moment, sniffing the air then pawing the ground. He shook his hump and then I realised that it had had a *banderilla* stuck in it, which looked like a small spear with decorations of some kind. Every now and then he would shake himself, trying to dislodge it. A roar went up as the first 'brave', or mad youth, jumped into the path of the bull. He looked about eighteen and wild-eyed. I was near enough to see that his eyes were red – probably from drink.

The bull charged him furiously and he got out of the way just in time. The bull turned, but his prey had climbed on to the stockade just out of reach. The bull then seemed to notice the multitude and ran round the stockade trying to get at legs and whatever else was sticking out. Another lad jumped into the ring with his mates.

Another charge – this time partially successful as one of the men went sprawling. He was picked up before the bull could turn on him. The huge beast could get up a speed but was too bulky to do tight manoeuvres and this was where a fit man might survive. The important words were 'might' and 'survive' because one of the bloods trying to show his superior bravery to the crowd went too near.

Unlike bullfights in Spain, this was not about killing the bull and I have to say that it gave me a certain pleasure to see these louts – as indeed they were – getting tossed out of the ring. Everyone knows the phrase 'tossed by a bull' but this was the first time I had ever seen it happen. The animal used the full force of his neck muscles and the man flew high in the air, cartwheeling as if in slow motion, right out of the corral, and landed in a heap outside.

He was dragged off. For some reason this caused outrage and sticks appeared with which the bull was struck every time he came near enough. It was utterly despicable. The cowards doing it were well out of harm's way above the animal's head. Every now and then a 'brave' would jump in, but after half an hour the bull was either tired or bored and another was substituted.

'At least they don't kill them,' I said to Eduardo.

'Pity,' he said, eyes bleary with alcohol. 'Much more interesting.' I realised that there was a huge cultural difference between us and said nothing, but I couldn't credit that a man with a love of animals who had worked with pets until quite recently could get any pleasure from seeing an animal tormented so. I was looking for an excuse to get out of this hellish scene.

The crowd started hissing. The new bull, it seemed, was

a bit of a coward. Or more intelligent, I thought. He didn't bother charging inaccessible people and didn't lose his cool. After a while he was driven back to the enclosed area behind the stockade to much cat-calling. It looked as though more betting was going on, maybe to do with the time that any particular man would last in the arena with the bull. Before the next bull was driven in, a mangy dog strolled into the centre of the arena.

At once a howl went up and thirty or more villagers jumped in, managing to corner him. He got several hefty clouts with sticks as he yelled in fear and tried to escape. Several blows later he was caught and physically thrown out of the corral. I had coped with the cockfight, I had coped with the bullfight, but this was more than I could stomach.

With the dog gone the crowd turned on themselves and an enthusiastic fight ensued, broken up by the arrival of a couple of policemen, who shot their guns into the air.

'I'm going to see if the dog is all right,' I said to Eduardo, glad to find an excuse to leave. I went off in search of the victim. I saw him running on three legs towards the centre of the village. At least he was alive but his wounds or injuries would have to heal themselves. I walked on back to the house and climbed into the hammock to rest. I knew that the night was going to be a long one and at this rate I was not going to catch Eduardo in either a sober or rational mood to broach the subject of my departure to England.

They came back later and nothing was said about my having left early. We took it in turns to use the cold shower and changed clothes. I had remembered to wash a couple of shirts and in this heat they were dry in half an hour. Then we set off for the evening's entertainment.

This was to consist of a meal and the village dance. There were ten of us at the restaurant and the mayor announced that

231

he was going to settle the bill as a gesture of his gratitude that we had come so far to his village. Danger had been settled down somewhere for the night in anticipation of a lot of noise. The band struck up while we were eating the main course – an ear-splitting din. Two trumpets, drums, guitars, bongo drums and a small guitar called a *tiple* made up the group, plus two singers, a man and a woman. It was ten-thirty.

Time had sped by and so far I had avoided too much drink. Eduardo was well away, though.

I was just drinking a coffee when one of the village girls grabbed me for a dance. She was plain, with a round face and a wide smile, and I soon found myself in the thick of it. The entire square had been taken over for the dancing and hundreds of couples were dancing to salsa-type music. The band was now in full swing. They never took a break and were capable of playing for hours on end. The girls held candles in the air as they danced and *aguardiente* was passed around for everyone to help themselves without needing to stop dancing.

After what must have been a couple of hours I was getting tired and drunk at the same time – it hadn't escaped the attention of the village that a gringo was among them. I had lost sight of Eduardo and his cronies and had given up the idea of slipping away for an early night. Every time I wanted to stop dancing another girl would grab me and the bottle would be passed to me. Things started to calm down at five – the girl with whom I was dancing suddenly darted away as a man staggered over and pushed me out of the way.

I went sprawling and looked up to see my attacker being held by a couple of his mates. I was vaguely aware of Eduardo standing over me and waving his gun threateningly. Suddenly it went off. This had the effect of making the men disperse and I staggered back to the house. It was all locked up – no sign of life whatsoever.

Feeling very woozy, I collapsed in the hammock and passed out.

The next thing I remembered was waking up in the back of the Land Rover feeling dreadful and bouncing about, which made things worse. The doctor looked at me and said, 'You will live.'

To my eyes he looked just as bad as I felt. I had had one *aguardiente* too many, and I made a resolution not to touch another drop. They had found me in the hammock mid-morning. I didn't ask what they had been up to – I was just grateful that they had found my things, including the *cédula*, and chucked them in the back with me. Eduardo was asleep on the other side of the back seat, snoring with his mouth open. It was not a pretty sight. He looked as if he was not going to come to for hours. Not that he needed to.

After what seemed an interminable time we got into Apartado at night. I collapsed into my bed and passed straight out for the second time in twenty-four hours. I didn't come to until ten the following morning. Eduardo was still asleep. I had the worst headache of my life and felt queasy with it. A cold shower only made it worse. I had the traditional Colombian *guayabo* – their word for hangover. To add to my misery the temperature rapidly climbed to the mid-forties and was very humid. The only thing drinkable in the house was beer.

I helped myself to one and tried sipping it slowly. My flight was due at one o'clock and I had two hours to kill before it left. I looked around for some writing paper, but there was none. I shook Eduardo, but he grunted and turned over to resume snoring. I packed my hold-all and set out for the main part of the village thinking a coffee might help. It didn't, but I met up with a taxi driver who offered to wait and run me to the airport for two hundred pesos – extortionate, probably, but I was in no mood to argue. I would have to write to Eduardo. Perhaps it would be easier that way.

There was no sign of the doctor or the mayor – perhaps they, too, were sleeping it off, but I would have liked to say goodbye to them. I felt slightly guilty as I arrived at the airstrip and joined the motley passengers who were going back to Medellín. I would write once I was back. Apartado was much like I imagined the Wild West to have been: bars, guns, hard drinking and horses. It had all been too much – I doubted that I would have survived two weeks there. I was looking forward to the cool air of Medellín and getting rid of this wretched *guayabo*.

The plane arrived spot on time, sending up a great dust storm as it landed. Only four passengers got off, and crossed themselves as they stood on land. We wasted no time in boarding. The captain warned us that there was a bit of turbulence and that the flight might take half an hour longer than usual. A nun sitting opposite me crossed herself and got down to reading the Bible.

We took off with a minimum of preliminaries and within minutes we were being tossed about. After one almighty bump the Bible shot out of the nun's hands, hit the roof of the plane and miraculously landed back in her hands. Without a word she continued reading. Through the cockpit door I could see that both pilots were busy. Out of the window I could see nothing but a green haze. I was feeling more and more sick. Just when I was starting to get desperate I saw clearer skies and mountains above us on both sides, signalling that we were flying up the Aburra valley into Medellín. I managed to damp down the nausea as we landed to the usual ripple of applause. As soon as I was walking to the terminal building I started to feel better. Maybe turbulence is a good cure for a hangover, I thought.

Chapter 18

'Dr David!'

I turned. Only one person called me that. Among the dark-haired young women standing where passengers emerged in the arrivals hall at Medellín airport, I spotted Cristina. She was shaking her hands. Something was obviously very wrong for her to have been out here.

'Señora Serrano, Señora Serrano,' she repeated, with more shaking of her hands.

Pilar. What was she up to now?

'She is a *bruja*.' This wasn't the first time Cristina had described Pilar as a witch.

We found a taxi for the short journey back. It seemed Pilar had a new friend. She'd appeared a few times before I left, but while I was away the two women had been holed up in the house in the afternoons.

'And they are talking about you, Dr David, and the microscope.' She paused and looked around the taxi to check that nobody was listening. 'And they are burning incense.' She sat back triumphant.

I wasn't worried about Pilar or her friend. Pilar wasn't a witch but she *was* a highly manipulative, greedy, duplicitous female. End of story.

But Hector was different. Cristina told me a terrifying story – if it was true. She had overheard the 'witches' talking about Hector's fiendish plans to deal with me once and for all. She had been quite convinced that I wouldn't be on the flight, that Hector had sent his henchmen to kidnap me – or worse. Like everyone else in Colombia, Cristina believed that as a gringo I had money. I might not have it here but I had it somewhere. Alternatively, someone who cared about me had money and would gladly hand it over if the option was a bullet in my head.

To calm her down I told her all about San Pedro and how Eduardo was in good spirits and that his divorce had come through. She didn't know whether to be pleased or sorry – pleased that he was finally free of the witch, or sorry, as a good Catholic, that his marriage vows were broken.

'So when will Dr Serrano come back to Medellín?' she asked.

I had to tell her that I didn't know. I didn't know because of course he didn't know that I was leaving. He didn't even know about the microscope. I told her that I hadn't been able to wake Eduardo and had left him sleeping off a monumental binge. But at the moment that wasn't what was on my mind. I couldn't have spent more than six daylight hours in Apartado, so if Hector's men were looking for me they would have had a hard job.

'Look, Cristina,' I went on, 'it's obvious that I'm going to have to leave – sooner rather than later. I'll need to write a letter to Eduardo so that he can make arrangements. Maybe he will come back.'

'Not while the *bruja* is still here.'

I had no idea on what grounds the divorce had been obtained or what the settlement might have been, but surely Pilar wouldn't be allowed to stay in the house. The clinic, after all, was Eduardo's livelihood.

The taxi stopped outside the clinic and we got out. 'Have there been many clients?' I asked.

'Quite a few, but they are all coming this week and Señora Schwarzkopf wants a visit this week to check Bosun.'

I laughed – nothing changes. 'I suppose I'd better tell her I'm going,' I said.

We went in the clinic and Cristina stopped dead. We could hear Pilar on the phone talking to Hector. We both froze and tried to listen – but she put down the phone after a minute.

'She's going out,' whispered Cristina, as the door leading to the house was shut. Sure enough a minute later we heard the main door close. We heaved a sigh of relief and went in. There was a smell of incense about the place. 'See?' whispered Cristina.

'Maybe she's just taken a liking to the smell,' I said, trying to joke, but the look on Cristina's face showed she was terrified.

I picked up a bundle of letters to me: a couple from England – Gloria was getting married and the whole family were going over later in the year. I was to be invited. There was one from Marta wanting to see me. 'I owe it to her,' I said aloud.

'What?' said Cristina, alarmed that I was talking to myself.

'Marta. She wants to see me,' I said.

Marta and Cristina had taken to each other and Cristina had persuaded me that I should see her to clear the air. She was right, of course: I hadn't made it clear that I did not want to get married.

I would also have to give notice to the Institute that I wouldn't be able to teach after the end of the month. Suddenly life seemed so much more complicated than it had been a few weeks ago. On the other hand, I missed home so much now that I couldn't wait to get back. Gloria had sent a photograph of her and her husband-to-be having a picnic somewhere in the Cotswolds. It was just so English and my mind flashed back to lazy days in Canterbury when I would park the car on the way back to the hospital and just walk, with the birds, the country smells, the soft grass under my feet. I gave notice to Jairo the next day.

'I'm sorry to see you go, *amigo*,' he said, shaking my hand. 'Maybe you can come back in a few years?'

I nodded. 'Maybe,' I said, with a smile, although I doubted it.

'You have to get a *paz y salvo* certificate, by the way,' he added.

'What's that?' I asked, alarm creeping into my voice.

'If you want to leave the country you have to get permission – and pay your taxes,' he explained.

More complications – but here Jairo turned out to be a useful *palanca*: the family accountant would help me fill in the form and calculate my tax. An afternoon's work would do it. As I had no evening classes, I ambled over to the Colombo-Americano library to spend a quiet hour reading. I had no desire to go back to the house. I relaxed and began to feel hungry.

Suddenly I saw a squat man with sunglasses looking my way. His face was vaguely familiar and as I went out he followed me. Then I recognised him: he was one of the DAS agents who had arrested me just after I got back from Cúcuta the second time. He touched my arm. 'Come with me. You are detained.' It happened so quickly I didn't have time to wonder how they knew where I was, and a few minutes later I found myself sitting in a cell in the DAS offices. But this time I didn't have to wait long: the chief of police hauled me out personally. He had Pilar with him and he began to question me about the microscope. I explained that we had agreed two months as a reasonable time for me to find two hundred dollars – I naturally omitted to say that I had no intention of paying anything. Pilar then launched into a tirade about how she didn't think I had any intention of paying, and insisted that I be locked up until such time that I came up with the cash. I could sense the chief wavering. From his point of view, locking me up was the easy option. 'May I make a phone call?' I asked politely.

They both took this as a positive sign: perhaps I was going to ring a friend and borrow the money. 'Of course,' said the chief, still without a smile but more conciliatory now.

I had taken to carrying a diary on me with important phone numbers and I flicked through it until I found Fernando Echavarria's number. I could hear Cristina's voice as clearly as if she was standing beside me. 'He is a superior judge. His brother is the governor of Antioquia,' she had told me, when he brought in his wife's Pekinese. Poppy had recovered well from her hysterectomy.

I phoned, praying that he would be in. My prayer was answered for Fernando himself answered the phone. After our time on the golf course, we were on first-name terms. I spoke to him in rapid English. He didn't appear fazed as I told my story. Meanwhile, my captors looked on, not understanding a word. He listened and asked what I had been charged with. I said that as far as I knew I hadn't committed any crime at all.

Fernando agreed. 'It's bluff and extortion. Let me talk to the chief,' he said.

I passed the phone. 'My lawyer,' I said.

It might not have been strictly accurate, but I knew no other lawyers in Colombia. The chief of police's expression changed when he realised who he was talking to. No, the Englishman was not under arrest. No, the British Consulate had not been informed – it was just a preliminary discussion and, of course, there was no intention whatsoever of detaining me. He put the phone back into my hand with an apologetic shrug and a nod in the direction of Pilar.

Fernando told me I was free to go but that I would be wise to make myself scarce for a few weeks.

'Thank you,' I said, 'I intend to do just that.'

I passed the phone back to the chief of police. 'The superior judge says I am free to go,' I said, 'so if you will excuse me?'

I stood up and, not looking at Pilar, walked quietly out into the street. I headed back to the Pasaje Junin, and quite by coincidence bumped into Marta. We hugged and the tears in her eyes made my conscience prick.

'Have you got time to eat something? We need to talk. When are you due back home?'

We had two hours – I cursed the chaperone system. We went to the same restaurant as always and I smiled wryly to myself as Marta poured me a beer while we looked at the menu. Although she knew there was no love lost between me and Pilar, the recent turn of events filled her with alarm. 'You must leave right away – this gangster Hector will be furious that you have beaten him this time.'

'I know. I have decided to get out, leave.' I paused. 'Next week. All I need is the *paz y salvo*.'

Marta said nothing. I hesitated and then went on, 'You know, seeing you with your family showed me that England would be a difficult place for you to feel *amañada*.' I used the *paisa* word for 'at home' to emphasise what I was getting at. 'Maybe if I was fabulously wealthy and you could come home twice a year it would work. But I'm hopeless at making money,' I said, speaking the absolute truth. 'And much as I love this country, I see no future here for me. It's helped me to see what I really want to do and that is work for the RSPCA.' I had tried to explain to her before what the

RSPCA was but it was an alien concept to her and she had never been interested in my life with animals.

'I could come and see if I like it,' she said.

'You think your father would let you out without being married?' I said, maybe a bit harshly.

Marta said nothing, then changed the subject. Suddenly she seemed to have got her spirit back. 'When you leave you should tell everyone that you are going to Bogotá and then come and stay at Doña Pepa's. At least that will throw Hector's dogs off the scent.'

I laughed. 'Well, aren't you the devious one?' But she was right: I needed to have a plan like that.

I didn't put it past Hector to have the airport watched. Leaving Medellín would be a game of bluff and double bluff.

We shared a taxi to Doña Pepa's and I went in for a *tinto*. Marta said she would discuss it with her aunt, but she didn't think there would be a problem.

The next day I talked it through with Cristina and set a leaving date – two weeks hence. That would give me enough time to say goodbye to some of the clients, arrange flights and write to Eduardo so that he could sort something out.

I felt guilty at leaving Cristina but it didn't seem that I had much choice. I had a week at the Institute to work, that meant six hours a day, and I would work at the clinic in the mornings. Via Maria, the maid, I gave the impression to Pilar that I would be around for at least another couple of months. I just had to pray that Hector wouldn't strike before then. I had no doubt that somehow I would be stopped from going home if they had wind of my leaving date. For the next week I came home as late as possible, eating in town with Marta or Ramón or both, and going straight to bed when I came back. The *paz y salvo* took a bit of organising – a whole morning going through my documents and accounts and paying a ludicrously small amount of tax, the equivalent of twenty pounds. The accountant couldn't believe how little I had earned.

Finally I had to queue up at the DAS offices to get the infamous certificate allowing me to leave. I kept a wary eye open for the heavy brigade but fortunately it was in a different part of the building so I didn't bump into any of my old adversaries. I sailed out clutching my certificate, feeling as though I had just escaped from jail.

That week I visited Janina and Bosun for the last time. I could sense that Janina was embarrassed by my previous visit but I made no mention of it and neither did she. I checked out Bosun: he was still the fittest dog I had ever seen. Perhaps it had something to do with his daily caviar intake. 'He'll live another ten years at least – I'm sure of it,' I said.

He was happy to lie on my feet as I sipped a glass of wine. I was going to miss these visits and especially the dog. 'Can I take him back with me to England?' I joked.

For a horrible moment I realised that I had said the wrong thing.

'Only if I come too,' Janina replied, her eyelashes batting.

'He would not have quite such a life of luxury,' I added hastily. 'And it rains all the time.'

Janina was busy pulling something from her desk. 'You've been good to Bosun – and I'll never forget how you saved his life.'

I thought this was going over the top, considering that I had removed a couple of teeth that had been coming out anyway.

'I want you to have this.' She passed me a hundred dollars in ten-dollar bills. 'It will liven up your trip home – you're going via Miami, I take it?'

¡Viva El Vet!

I hesitated to tell her that was so. But it was true. I was going to see Gloria 1, who had recently sent me her address.

'You'll find it more than enough to stay in Miami Beach for a week.'

I thanked her, put it into my pocket and asked her to ring for a taxi. I was not going to subject myself to a trip on public transport with a fortune in my pocket. A hundred dollars was a huge amount of money – half the price of my life, if Hector's arithmetic was anything to go by. I looked around at the sumptuous luxury in which Janina lived and felt a twinge of sadness for her. I realised I knew so little about her life and how she had come to live here.

A hoot announced the arrival of the taxi, and I walked out through the garden. When I glanced back, Bosun was staring after me eagerly, as if waiting for a signal to join me. I knew that he would have bounded out if I had so much as raised my hand. As we drove off his mistress was nowhere to be seen.

Back at the clinic I gave half of the money to Cristina – it was the equivalent of a couple of months' wages and would act as a cushion until Eduardo took the reins again, as I was sure he would.

I spent my last pay packet from the Institute on a meal with Ramón, Marta and Cristina. Doña Pepa had agreed to let me stay that night at her house and over dinner – at the same restaurant to which Eduardo had taken me on my first night in Medellín overlooking the Pasaje Junin – the escape plan was hatched. I would have to leave suddenly, with no warning and very early in the morning, in case Pilar got wind of it or discovered me leaving.

Ramón volunteered to pick me up at the end of the road. Pilar would assume that I was on the next flight to Bogotá and no doubt Hector would send someone to the airport to intercept me. I had no doubt whatsoever that I would be

243

kidnapped if I stuck around too long. All three warned me
that this wasn't a game and that I would have to be careful.

'These guys mean business,' Ramón added, as he handed
me my new pinstripe suit. For ten dollars, it was the best suit
I had ever owned and I clutched it to me as we strolled down
the Pasaje Junin for the last time.

I suddenly felt sad that I was leaving. It had been the most
adventurous year of my life – and one that would shape
things for the rest of it. I had made more friends in one
year than in the previous ten. I had learned that I couldn't
stomach working with pets in a country that had children
living in appalling conditions, which made things difficult
for a while on my return home – until I had thought things
through. Having experienced culture shock on my arrival, I
didn't realise that I was about to go through it again. But,
all things considered, I loved the country and I was feeling
tearful as we got into a bus to travel up to Doña Pepa's house.
Some *quesito* and *bocadillo* revived me, and I listened to
Doña Pepa worrying about the danger I was in.

In my passport I had a ticket to Cali. The plan was that I
would spend a week there with Bertica's family until the hue
and cry that my leaving would cause in some quarters had
subsided, then fly out on Sunday week on the daily flight
from Cali to Miami. It was the day that my *paz y salvo* ran
out so I was cutting things a bit fine.

My last day at the clinic was quiet – Eduardo would have
had my letter by now and although I would have preferred
to have heard from him, he would surely come back soon. I
couldn't risk staying another night. We had timed everything
down to the nth degree. Pilar was in the house but had sent me
to Coventry. I cursed my luck as she showed signs of staying
in on my last night – I had hoped she'd be out on the town
with Hector.

¡Viva El Vet!

I came in at ten, and as she was in her room alone I crept into Maria's room to say goodbye to Ian David, again feeling tearful. What would become of him?

Maria had made me some *arepas* to take with me and shook my hand with tears running down her face. I just hoped Pilar didn't notice. But that wasn't likely: Maria was little more than a slave and slaves don't have emotions – Pilar wouldn't notice.

I packed quietly and settled down to try to sleep. The alarm went off at six, sounding like a siren. Would it have woken Pilar? Feeling sick I got dressed, picked up my things and slipped quietly out of the front door. I thought I had got away with it until I heard a furious knocking on the window and looked up to see an equally furious face glaring down at me. It was Pilar. I heard her yelling as I hurried to the end of the street where I hoped Ramón would be waiting for me. 'We will stop you,' she shouted, or words to that effect. I congratulated myself grimly on my knowledge of Colombian obscenities before I arrived at the main *avenida*. There, as arranged, was my good friend Ramón who had borrowed a car for the express purpose of getting me away as fast as possible. We sped away and ten minutes later we were having breakfast at Doña Pepa's. I noticed that Ramón had broken out in a sweat and suddenly realised that he was risking his neck. I would have to lie low for a day and a night before taking the trip to the airport to pick up the Cali flight. He and I said our goodbyes. I would take a taxi to the airport.

'Hey, good knowin' ya, *amigo*. See y' round.'

But I wouldn't see him around. I wondered if he would ever escape the poverty of his homeland and find his way back to New York, where his dreams of fortune lay.

That night I lay on a settee in Doña Pepa's lounge. The old lady had allowed Marta and me to be together longer than usual. She probably sensed that we weren't about to abuse her hospitality. Outside I could hear the noises of the city. I tried to isolate them: in that way perhaps I would remember them. I might never hear them again. My mind wound back over the year – not quite a year: it would be summer when I got back to England if all went according to plan. I would never forget the hospitality and generosity of these people, whether rich, like Gloria's and Bertica's families, or poor, Doña Pepa, Cristina and Maria.

I had told my family that I was going off on an adventure and when I set off I had no idea just how much of an adventure Colombia would turn out to be, complete with guns, gangsters, monkeys, parrots. When I woke up in the morning now, my first thoughts were in Spanish. I even dreamed in Spanish. This was a prize beyond measure, which would give my life an extra dimension for years to come. Eventually even Medellín seemed to close down for the night and I fell into a troubled sleep. It was not over yet.

The following day I didn't move from the house until the taxi came for me. Dan had given me a copy of *Cien Años de Soledad – A Hundred Years of Solitude –* by Gabriel Garcia Marquez, in Spanish, which I read in the courtyard of Doña Pepa's house as she bustled around, offering me a non-stop supply of *tintos* while she prepared a celebration meal for my last evening in Medellín. I thought with sadness that the place I should be was the Pasaje Junin, in the upstairs bar, clapping my hands for service, Marta pouring my beer and afterwards strolling with everybody else, on the lookout for *gamines*, distracted by the occasional whispered '*bizcocho*'. But Doña Pepa had done her niece and me proud. And Marta even brought back a bottle of wine from town, although she and her aunt drank milk with their meal. The wine was for me.

No one came with me to the airport: it was better that way.

¡Viva El Vet!

Marta and I had said our goodbyes. Tender and tearful on both our parts. She was a lovely girl, a really lovely girl, and had things been different . . . who knows?

I had booked an early flight: Hector and his hoods were night people I reckoned and would be safely tucked up in bed. But it was still a nerve-racking experience.

At Cali airport I was met by Bertica's sister. She was very Europeanised and, with her, I felt I had already left. It was a quiet few days.

My next stop was Miami and Gloria 1. I would have time to talk everything over with someone who would understand. I sensed already that no one in England would be very interested; they had their own concerns.

I would soon discover that for most people South America was the music and glamour. And that's what they wanted to hear about, not the squalor and the poverty.

For me it had been a real watershed. Finding myself in the middle of this alien culture had led me to question everything, right down to whether it was right to be a vet.

The answer of course, was yes. But not there. For a year or so I had been all at sea. But my time in Colombia changed my life for the better. It gave me values I didn't have before. I met the kind of people I had never met before whose warmth and hospitality in the face of real adversity was hard to believe, people who had had to overcome far more than I ever had or would.

Going to Colombia had been something I just felt I had to do. As the jet took off from Cali, I looked to the future with complete optimism. Colombia had been such an adventure – I wouldn't have missed it for anything.

Postscript

On returning to England I went into private practice in London's King's Road. At the beginning I decided not to write to Eduardo or Cristina in case the mail was intercepted by Hector. Then, about six months later, Cristina wrote to me with sad news: Eduardo had been found dead in Apartado – gunshot wounds. Suicide, accident or foul play, nobody could decide. Although he was always reckless with the Beretta and he wasn't a happy man, I suspect that he was murdered. Life is cheap in Colombia, even if you are a vet.

There was even more tragedy to come. Gustavo, Gloria's brother-in-law, was shot dead at an armed hold-up. He had been driving along a road patrolled by bandits who put up roadblocks and demanded money. He decided to drive through it so they shot him.

As for Ian David, he would be twenty-five now and I have been a terrible godparent. Now that I am a parent myself, I think of him often. But, as Colombia should have taught me, thinking is not enough. Since I left Medellín, it has become the drug capital of the world. I would love to go back but my friends warn me it's too risky: kidnapping and armed hold-ups are not uncommon. But I keep hoping that one day I'll be able to return.